A Computer Model
of
Transformational
Grammar

MATHEMATICAL LINGUISTICS AND AUTOMATIC LANGUAGE PROCESSING

●

A GROUP OF
MONOGRAPHS
and
TEXTBOOKS

●

GENERAL EDITOR:
David G. Hays
State University
of New York
at Buffalo

A Computer Model
of
Transformational
Grammar

JOYCE FRIEDMAN

The University of Michigan
Ann Arbor, Michigan

with **Thomas H. Bredt · Robert W. Doran**
Bary W. Pollack · Theodore S. Martner

American Elsevier Publishing Company, Inc.

NEW YORK · 1971

AMERICAN ELSEVIER PUBLISHING COMPANY, INC.
52 Vanderbilt Avenue, New York, N.Y. 10017

ELSEVIER PUBLISHING COMPANY, LTD.
Barking, Essex, England

ELSEVIER PUBLISHING COMPANY
335 Jan Van Galenstraat, P.O. Box 211
Amsterdam, The Netherlands

International Standard Book Number 0-444-00084-4

Library of Congress Card Number 77-127770

Printed in the United States of America

FOR ELEANOR AND HARRY

Contents

Preface

This book describes a model of transformational grammar developed for use on a computer. The model is embodied in a computer system that serves as a computational aid to the linguist in his role as writer of grammars of natural languages. The programs accept grammars in roughly the form suggested in Noam Chomsky's *Aspects of the Theory of Syntax* and provide, as output, information which makes it easier to achieve coherent and satisfactory grammars.

To write the programs, we first needed a consistent theory of transformational grammar, with a precise format for writing grammars, and a clear statement of the algorithms by which sentences are derived. We found no description of grammar sufficiently detailed or rigorous to serve as the basis for a computer system and therefore undertook to develop a formal model of transformational grammar. As the computer system progressed, changes were made and details filled in. The result is a rigorous and consistent interpretation of the original theory presented by Chomsky.

The model consists of a format for grammars and algorithms for deriving sentences. The unique features of the model and the system include a formal description of the syntax of transformational grammar, a phrase-structure generation scheme which enables the user to direct an otherwise random generation process towards interesting trees, a complete format for the lexicon and a lexical insertion algorithm, a unified treatment of **lexical insertion** and transformations, and a language for specifying the traffic rules of a grammar.

In the model there is some freedom to make theoretical choices among well-defined alternatives. Consequently, it is flexible enough to adapt to a range of possibilities within the theory of transformational grammar. It has been the basis of computer-tested grammars of French, Old English, English, Japanese, the American Indian language Serrano, and the Persian dialect Vafsi-Tati. The model has also proved useful in teaching the basic ideas of generative grammar.

The basis for this book was a series of reports prepared while the authors were at Stanford University. The book was prepared later while I was at the University of Michigan. I should like to express my thanks to Yves Ch. Morin, who capably solved many problems and cheerfully performed many chores which would have fallen to my co-authors had they not been in California or London. Mr. Morin has also kindly allowed us to use, as Appendix A, parts of his grammar of French.

Many users of the computer system contributed suggestions for improvements to the system and to this description of it. I should like to thank those users collectively, and to thank specially my colleagues Kenneth C. Hill and Michael A. H. O'Malley. From earlier times, I am grateful to Donald E. Walker, who suggested to me that linguistics might be interesting, and to Barbara Hall Partee, for many conversations on transformational grammar.

The research was supported in part by the United States Air Force Electronics Systems Division under Contract F19628-C-0035, and by The National Science Foundation under Grant GS-2771. I take this opportunity to thank project monitors J. Bruce Fraser of ESD and Murray Aborn of NSF.

Partial descriptions of the system appeared earlier in two papers in the *Communications of the ACM,* 12 (1969), 40-46 and 341-348. The ACM has granted permission for use of the figures from those papers, which appear in Chapters 5 and 6.

Finally, I would like to thank the series editor, David G. Hays, for his painstaking critical reading of the manuscript.

Joyce Friedman

South Salem, New York
August 1970

CHAPTER 1

Introduction

A transformational grammar is an explicit formal specification of a language.
Its explicit nature has led some people to believe that a desire to use computers
motivated the development of the theory. Historically, this belief has no basis.
Nonetheless, an important consequence of the formal nature of transformational
grammars is that it is natural to use a computer to work with them.

BACKGROUND

In this book we describe a computer model of grammar, based on the linguistic
theories of Noam Chomsky. The model is the outcome of a project entitled
"Computer Aids to Linguistic Research." Our original goal was to construct a
system of computer programs to help linguists write and test transformational
grammars for natural language syntax. The programs were to accept a
grammar as data, make error checks, generate sentences, and in general
provide outputs to help the writer of the grammar understand how it was
working, and thus enable him to improve it.

Computer assistance in grammar writing is needed because writing a transformational grammar is intrinsically difficult. The linguist must first understand what is going on in the language, but he also has many purely technical
problems in making the grammar describe the observed phenomena. A rule of
grammar may behave as intended in isolation, but in the grammar it must
interact properly with all other rules. Thus, the linguist needs to consider the
grammar as a whole; he needs not only a "rule-tester," but a "grammar-tester."

Complete specification is necessary for a computer model. We found that
existing models of grammar, while formal by comparison with previous work in
linguistics, were relatively informal compared to what is needed for a computer
model. We thus became primarily involved in formalizing a precise notion of
transformational grammar. Although we were led to this formalization by the
demands of the computer, formalization is also of linguistic importance, as
Chomsky has often stressed. For example, questions of relative simplicity of
grammars are answerable only when some precise notational scheme makes the
grammars comparable. Even more important, a grammar cannot be said to
define a language unless the process of sentence generation is fully specified, so
that sentences are generated in a well-defined way, without appeal to intuition.

Our work thus produced not only the computer system originally proposed, but
also a formal model of transformational grammar. We use the phrase
"computer model" to refer to the combination of this formal model of grammar
and the computer programs that implement it. The model provides a notation

for grammars and specifies the algorithms by which a grammar generates sentences. The notation is itself described in a formal metalanguage. The algorithms are described both in English for the readers of this book and in a programming language for the computer.

LINGUISTIC THEORY

The theory of transformational grammar, as presented by Noam Chomsky in *Aspects of the Theory of Syntax* (1965), underlies our model. (That book is familiarly known as *Aspects,* and we so refer to it.) We view our model as an interpretation of the theory presented in *Aspects*. However, as will be seen, we deviate from it in many respects: we have needed to make our model more precise, and we have felt free to generalize in order to make our model flexible.

Where *Aspects* suggests an approach, but fails to provide details, we have supplied them. Major examples here are the lexical insertion algorithm, and the control language developed to implement the "traffic rules" for transformations.

Where Chomsky says "Suppose A," we have often made it possible for the user either to "suppose A" or to "suppose not A," so that the consequences can be explored. For example, the order of lexical insertion can be varied by the user, and the principle of strict local subcategorization is optional.

Where conventions seem arbitrary or are not fully defined, we have chosen those which unify and simplify the model. Thus, the notations and conventions for subcategorization features and selectional features are the same; the notation for these features is in turn very close to that for the structural description of a transformation, which itself is a natural extension of the representation of a tree.

Our ideas have also been influenced by examples of transformational grammars, primarily the MITRE grammar (Zwicky *et al.*, 1965), the IBM Core grammar (Rosenbaum and Lochak, 1966), and the UCLA working papers on English syntax (Stockwell *et al.*, 1967). The formalism of our model was made general enough so that those grammars could be expressed naturally. However, we did not feel it necessary to include peculiar features of individual grammars which did not seem consistent with the rest of the theory or which seemed to be instances of some more general but unstated concept.

As a consequence of its generality, the model has been able to accommodate a wide variety of grammars—ranging from several based literally on *Aspects,* to a modified case grammar, to some grammars incorporating ideas and techniques from the recent developments sometimes called "generative semantics."

Linguistic theory is currently in a period of rapid change. Some of the decisions made in designing the model have turned out to be particularly good in the light of recent developments. For example, the deep structure constraints of Perlmutter (1968) can be expressed as contextual features without change to the system. We anticipate that the modular construction of the system will make it relatively easy to investigate proposals for interleaving lexical and transformational rules. Other recent developments will not be so easily treated, and we are well aware that constant change will be required to keep the model current.

HISTORICAL NOTE

The earliest computer systems for transformational grammar were those of
Petrick (1965) and the MITRE Corporation (Zwicky *et al.*, 1965; Friedman, 1965).
Both were approaches to the analysis or parsing problem for grammars based
on a pre-*Aspects* theory.

Lieberman (1966) and Blair (1966) made the first attempt to program a model
based on *Aspects*. Later, at the same time as we were developing our model,
Gross (1967; 1968) and Londe and Schoene (1968) developed on-line rule-testers
for transformational grammars. The problems best treated by a system
designed for immediate response to a user at a console differ from those appropriate to an off-line system such as ours, so that although there is some over-
lap in the treatment of transformations, the systems are very different.

PLAN OF THIS BOOK

In one sense this entire book is a definition of transformational grammar. The
most logical way to present this definition would be to begin with the basic
concepts of tree, complex symbol, analysis, restriction, and structural change,
and the corresponding operations. The basic concepts could then be used in
defining the three components of a grammar: phrase structure, lexicon, and
transformations. Finally, the component algorithms could be presented.

We deviate from the logical order of presentation and instead give the model
component by component, in order to enable the reader to see an application of
each basic concept as soon as it is introduced. This order will also make it
possible to read the discussion of a single component without having studied all
previous material.

Each basic concept is presented just prior to the component with which it is
most closely associated. This necessitates some cross-references and occasionally some forward references. For example, we discuss trees with the
phrase structure component and complex symbols with the lexical component,
even though complex symbols do occur in trees.

To help the reader understand the system as a whole, we begin in Chapter 2
with an example of a transformational grammar containing all three components.
This example will be most meaningful to readers familiar with some notation
for grammars. Other readers may prefer to skim the example and to return to
it as the parts of a grammar are discussed. A more complete version of this
example appears as Appendix A.

In Chapter 3 we introduce the formal metalanguage used for describing the
syntax of grammars. This metalanguage is used throughout the book and for
the summary of syntax given in Appendix B.

Chapters 4 and 5 present the basic concept of tree and the phrase structure
component. The algorithm for this component is designed to generate
"interesting" trees.

Chapters 6 and 7 present the basic concept of complex symbol and the lexical
component. The lexical insertion process has not previously been described in
detail; we give for the first time a complete algorithm.

Chapters 8 and 9 present the basic concepts of analysis, restriction, and structural change, and the transformational component. Various proposals have been made for controlling the order of application of transformations; a unique feature of our model is that the specification of the algorithm for transformation order is included as part of the grammar.

Finally, in the last chapter we discuss the computer program and some computer experiments in transformational grammar.

CHAPTER 2

Overview

Before beginning the detailed discussion of the computer model, we present an example that illustrates both the notation for grammars and the use of the programs. It consists of a small grammar of French and a sample derivation. Each part is presented twice, first as originally prepared by Querido (1969) at the University of Montreal, and then as redone in the computer system. The grammar has been greatly reduced by selecting only those transformations used in the derivation of the sample sentence.

PHRASE STRUCTURE

Figure 1 gives the phrase structure rules as written by the French linguists; Figure 2 gives them as prepared for input to the computer system. The computer form begins with the comment "MONTREAL FRENCH"; all material within quotation marks is ignored by the program. PHRASESTRUCTURE and $END delimit the phrase structure component.

The rewriting symbol for the phrase structure rules is the equal-sign, and each rule ends with a period. The computer form is a linearization of the usual form, with both parentheses (options) and braces (choices) represented by parentheses. No ambiguity arises from this double use of parentheses, because the presence of a comma distinguishes the choices from the options. The phrase structure rules have been reordered so that the rule that expands SN (noun phrase) comes after all rules that introduce SN. The other differences are all minor: the symbol Δ has been replaced by DELTA, the symbol P (proposition) has been changed to English S (sentence), and accents have been omitted.

LEXICON

Figure 3 is a listing of a partial lexicon. This component is present implicitly in the original French grammar, where vocabulary words and complex symbols are indicated in base trees. The lexicon first defines the three sets of features: category, inherent, and contextual. Category features identify the nodes at which lexical items are inserted; the list determines the order of insertion. Inherent features occur in complex symbols in the lexicon, and are also added by transformations. Contextual features determine the context in which a vocabulary word can appear. A positively specified contextual feature indicates an environment that *must* be present; a negative specification one that *must not* be present. The lexicon defines these features by giving a structural analysis of the context; the word is inserted at the location indicated by the underline symbol ( ). For

P $\rightarrow$ # (PRE) SN PRED #

PRE $\rightarrow$ (INT) (NEG)

NEG $\rightarrow$ ne pas

PRED $\rightarrow$ $\begin{Bmatrix} \text{SV (ADV}_{\text{INST}}) \\ \text{SA} \end{Bmatrix}$

ADV$_{\text{INST}}$ $\rightarrow$ par $\begin{Bmatrix} \text{SN} \\ \Delta \end{Bmatrix}$

SV $\rightarrow$ V (COMPL)

SA $\rightarrow$ COP ADJ (COMPL)

COP $\rightarrow$ est

SN $\rightarrow$ $\begin{Bmatrix} \text{(SN) P} \\ \text{(DET) N} \end{Bmatrix}$

COMPL $\rightarrow$ $\begin{Bmatrix} \text{SN} \\ \text{P} \end{Bmatrix}$ (SN)

DET $\rightarrow$ $\left(\begin{Bmatrix} \text{DEF} \\ \text{quel} \end{Bmatrix} \right)$ (CARD)

DEF $\rightarrow$ $\begin{Bmatrix} \text{ANAPH} \\ \text{DEM} \end{Bmatrix}$

ANAPH $\rightarrow$ $\begin{Bmatrix} \text{ce} \left(\begin{Bmatrix} \text{ci} \\ \text{là} \end{Bmatrix} \right) \\ \text{le} \end{Bmatrix}$

DEM $\rightarrow$ ce $\left(\begin{Bmatrix} \text{ci} \\ \text{là} \end{Bmatrix} \right)$

CARD $\rightarrow$ $\begin{Bmatrix} \text{SING} \\ \text{PLUR} \end{Bmatrix}$

SING $\rightarrow$ un

PLUR $\rightarrow$ $\begin{Bmatrix} \text{PRO-CARD} \\ \text{quelques} \\ \text{deux} \\ \text{trois} \underline{} \end{Bmatrix}$

PRO-CARD $\rightarrow$ nombre de

Figure 1. Phrase structure rules

```
"MONTREAL FRENCH"

PHRASESTRUCTURE

S          = # (PRE) SN PRED # .
PRE        = (INT) (NEG) .
NEG        = NE PAS .
PRED       = (SV (ADVINS), SA) .
ADVINS     = PAR (SN, DELTA) .
SV         = V (COMPL) .
SA         = COP ADJ (COMPL) .
COP        = EST .
COMPL      = (SN, S) (SN) .
SN         = ((SN) S, (DET) N) .
DET        = ((DEF, QUEL)) (CARD) .
DEF        = (ANAPH, DEM) .
ANAPH      = (CE ((CI, LA)), LE) .
DEM        = CE ((CI, LA)) .
CARD       = (SING, PLUR) .
SING       = UN .
PLUR       = (PROCARD, QUELQUES, DEUX, TROIS) .
PROCARD    = NOMBRE DE .

       $END
```

Figure 2. Phrase structure, rewritten

example, common nouns are marked +NCOM, where NCOM = ⟨SN ⟨DET _⟩⟩; they can occur only following a determiner (DET) in a noun phrase (SN).

After the preliminary definitions, the lexicon contains the lexical entries. An entry may contain several vocabulary words that have the same complex symbols. The first entry here, for example, contains four words with one complex symbol. The computer form is completely free with respect to additional blanks, card boundaries, and position within the first 72 columns of a card. Thus, although the first entry occupies two lines, it is as if it were written all on one line.

In a computer derivation of a sentence, lexical items are selected at random from those in the lexicon that (i) are of the appropriate category, (ii) match inherent features already in the tree, and (iii) have contextual features satisfied by the tree.

TRANSFORMATIONS

Figures 4 and 5 present the transformational component. In the computer version a transformation consists of three parts: identification (TRANS), structural description (SD), and structural change (SC). The identification contains the number and name of the transformation, plus information used in determining when to invoke it. This information includes a group number (here I, II, or III), repetition parameters (here AACC, or AC, by default), optionality (here OB, by default), and keywords (e.g., (PAR DELTA) for transformation 7). The structural description is similar to the usual form, but we allow subanalysis to any depth. Terms in the structural description have numbers only for later reference. The conditions on transformations given in

```
LEXICON

"F E A T U R E      D E F I N I T I O N S"

CATEGORY      N  V  COP  ADJ .

INHERENT      PERS  TWOPERS  FEM  PLUR  HUM  MOI  NOMIN  TOI  ASN
              INF  DASHOUE  DEINF  R  SUBJ  PRENOM  PRON  FUTUR
              PROG  PRET  PASSIF  F .

CONTEXTUAL

              NCOM  = <SN<DET _ >>,
              TRAN  = <PRED/< _ SN(ADVINS) >>,
              DEUXTR = <PRED/< _ SN SN (ADVINS) >> .

"L E X I C A L      E N T R I E S"

ENTRIES

TRUDEAU  JEAN  ALCESTE
DEGAULLE  |+N  -PERS  -TWOPERS  -FEM  -PLUR  -NCOM|,
CELIMENE  |+N  -PERS  -TWOPERS  +FEM  -PLUR  -NCOM|,
LIVRE  |+N  -PERS  -TWOPERS  +FEM  -PLUR  +NCOM|,
PROFESSEUR  |+N  -PERS  -TWOPERS  -FEM  -PLUR  +NCOM|,
MOI  |+N  +MOI  +PERS  -TWOPERS  -FEM  -PLUR  -NCOM|,
JOLI  |+ADJ  +PRENOM|,
LEVE  SOURIR  CROIT  DANSE  BERNE  |+V|,
ACCEPTE  |+V  *FUTUR  *PROG  *PRET|,
REGARDE  RENCONTRE  |+V  *PRET  *FUTUR  *PROG|,
VOIR  |+V  +TRAN  *PRET  *FUTUR  *PROG|,
DONNE  |+V  +DEINF  +DEUXTR  *PRET  *FUTUR  *PROG|,
EST  |+COP  *PRET  *FUTUR  *PROG|.

    $ END
```

Figure 3. Lexicon

the original version are unnecessary in our format; however, the model does allow conditions.

Representation of the structural change by a sequence of elementary operations removes any possible ambiguity from the statement. In addition to adjunction, substitution, and deletion, the computer model provides several elementary operations that alter complex symbols. For example, |+PASSIF| MERGEF 4 adds a new feature specification to the complex symbol of term 4. |*FEM *PLUR| MOVEF 4 7 changes two features of term 7 so that they are the same as in term 4.

The last section of the transformational component in Figure 5 specifies the order of application of the transformations. In our model these "traffic rules" are an explicit part of a grammar. The supplementary transformation LOWESTS simply selects the lowest sentence with boundaries; it has no structural change. The control program (CP) specifies that the cyclic transformations (group I) apply in the lowest sentence. At the end of a cycle the boundaries are erased (by ELLIPSE), and the next highest sentence becomes lowest. After the last cycle, the tree is output, and the postcyclic transformations (group II) apply.

[T7]   POST -SUJ   OBL

#	(PRE)	SN	V	SN	(SN)	par	Δ	#	
1	2	3	4	5	6	7	8	9	=>
1	2	8	4	5	6	7	3	9	

[T9]   ANTEP-OBL   OBL

#	(PRE)	Δ	V	SN	(SN)	par+SN	#	
1	2	3	4	5	6	7	8	=>
1	2	5	4<+passif	$\emptyset$	6	7	8	

[T13]   AC-PRED   OBL

#	(PRE)	[(DET)	$\begin{bmatrix} \alpha\text{fem} \\ \alpha\text{pers} \\ \alpha 2\ \text{pers} \\ \alpha\text{plur} \end{bmatrix}_N$	(P)]$_{SN}$	(COP)	$\begin{Bmatrix} V \\ ADJ \end{Bmatrix}$
1	2	3	4	5	6	7
					Z	#
					8	9 =>
1	2	3	4	5	6	7<αfem αpers α2 pers αplur
					8	9

COND: 7 ⊲αfem
            αpers
            α2 pers
            αplur

[T33]   ELLIPSE ##   OBL

#	X	#	
1	2	3	=>
$\emptyset$	2	$\emptyset$	

Figure 4. Transformations

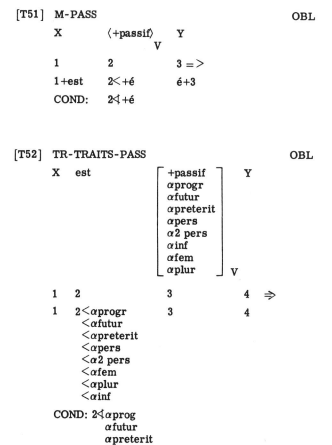

[T51] M-PASS   OBL

[T52] TR-TRAITS-PASS   OBL

Figure 4. Transformations (continued)

TRANSFORMATIONS

"CYCLIC TRANSFORMATIONS"

TRANS 7 POSTSUJ I (PAR DELTA).
  SD # (PRE) 3 SN V SN (SN) PAR 8 DELTA #.
  SC 8 ADRIS 3, 3 SUBSE 8.

TRANS 9 ANTEPOBL (DELTA PAR).
  SD # (PRE) 3 DELTA 4 V 5 SN (SN) PAR SN #.
  SC 5 SUBSE 3, |+PASSIF| MERGEF 4.

TRANS 13 ACPRED AACC.
  SD # (PRE) SN/<(DET) 4 N (S)> (COP) 7 (V,ADJ) % #.
  SC |*FEM *PERS *TWOPERS *PLUR| MOVEF 4 7.

TRANS 33 ELLIPSE.
  SD 1 # % 3 #.
  SC ERASE 1, ERASE 3.

"POSTCYCLIC TRANSFORMATIONS"

TRANS 51 MPASS II AACC.
  SD % 2 V|+PASSIF| %.
  SC EST ALESE 2, |+E| MERGEF 2, E ARISE 2.

TRANS 52 TRTRPA AACC (EST V).
  SD % 2 EST 3 V|+PASSIF| %.
  SC |*PROG *FUTUR *PRET *PERS *TWOPERS *FEM *PLUR *INF| MOVEF 3 2.

"SUPPLEMENTARY TRANSFORMATION FOR CONTROL PROGRAM"

TRANS LOWESTS III (#).
  SD 1 S ¬/<% S<# % #> %>, WHERE 1 DOM #.

"CONTROL PROGRAM"

CP   IN LOWESTS(1) DO <I>; TREE: II.

$END

Figure 5. Transformations, rewritten

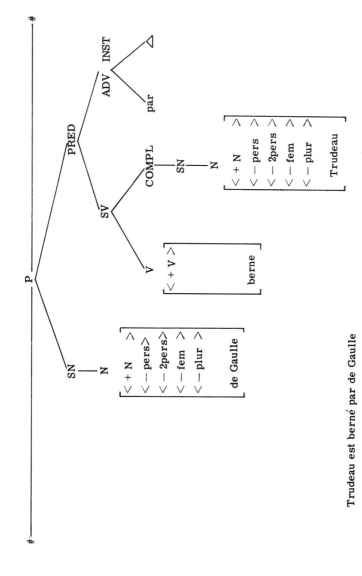

Trudeau est berné par de Gaulle

Figure 6. Base tree

```
"TRUDEAU EST BERNE PAR DEGAULLE."
    S      #
           SN    N
           PREC  SV     V
                        COMPL SN      N
                 ADVINSPAR
                        DELTA
           #
```

```
S<# SN<N> PRED<SV<V COMPL<SN<N>>> ADVINS<PAR DELTA>> #>.
```

Figure 7. Alternative forms of base tree

TRANSFORMATION

CYCLIQUE

7- POST-SUJ

$[\Delta [[\text{berne}]_V [\text{Trudeau}]_N \text{ par } [\text{de Gaulle}]_N]_{PRED}]_P$

9- ANTEP-OBJ

$[[\text{Trudeau}]_N [\begin{bmatrix} \langle +pass \rangle \\ \text{berne} \end{bmatrix}_V \text{ par } [\text{de Gaulle}]_N]_{PRED}]_P$

13- AC-PRED

$[\begin{bmatrix} \langle -plur \rangle \\ \langle -fem \rangle \\ \langle -pers \rangle \\ \langle -2pers \rangle \\ \text{Trudeau} \end{bmatrix}_N \begin{bmatrix} \langle -plur \rangle \\ \langle -fem \rangle \\ \langle -pers \rangle \\ \langle -2pers \rangle \\ \text{berne} \end{bmatrix}_V \text{ par } [\text{de Gaulle}]_N]_P$

POST-CYCLIQUE

51- M-PASS

$[[\text{Trudeau}]_N \text{ est } \begin{bmatrix} \langle +é \rangle \\ \text{berne} \end{bmatrix}_V \text{ é par } [\text{de Gaulle}]_N]_P$

Figure 8. Derivation

```
TRANSFORMATIONS WHICH HAVE APPLIED ARE

        1      7   LOWESTS
        2      1   POSTSUJ
        3      2   ANTEOBL
        4      3   ACPRED
        5      4   ELLIPSE
        6      5   MPASS
        7      6   TRTRPA


"TROJLEAU EST BERAE PAR DEGAULLE."

     1 ?   4 SN    10 N      16 ALCESTE
           5 PRED  6 SV      19 EST
                             7 V      17 REGARDE
                             20 E
           11 ADVINS  12 PAR        15 CELIMENE
                      3 SN    4 N

NODE  1   N
      1 +N -PERS -TWOPERS -FEM -PLUR -<SN<DET_>>|

NODE  1?  EST
      1 -PERS -TWOPERS -FEM -PLUR -FUTUR -PROG -PRETI

NODE  7   V
      1 +V -PERS -TWOPERS -FEM -PLUR -FUTUR -PROG -PPET +PASSIF +E|

NODE  4   N
      1 +N -PERS -TWOPERS +FEM -PLUR -<SN<DET_>>|

      ALCESTE EST REGARDE E PAR CELIMENE
```

Figure 9. Result of computer derivation

TREES

A tree used as an example in the reference appears in Figures 6 and 7. In the original version the tree contains complex symbols and vocabulary words. We have omitted them from the computer versions, so the program selects them from the lexicon.

Figure 7 illustrates two alternative ways of writing a tree, a tabular format and a bracketed linear form. Either of these is acceptable to the program (although it must be told which to expect.) The sentence at the top of the figure is a title for the tree; the program does not process it.

DERIVATION

The original derivation of "Trudeau est berne é par de Gaulle" is given in Figure 8. Figure 9 is the final part of the computer output for the input tree of Figure 7. The lexical insertion algorithm has randomly selected the words "Alceste," "regarde," and "Celimene," leading to the sentence "Alceste est regarde e par Celimene." If the words "Trudeau," "berne," and "de Gaulle" had been entered as part of the input tree, the program would have added their complex symbols and obtained the original result.

The program provides considerably more output than is shown in Figure 9. At each step of the derivation a message is printed. The tree is output when input, before and after lexical insertion, and, as shown, when the derivation is complete.

CHAPTER 3

Metalanguage

Linguists customarily choose a natural language as the metalanguage in which to describe transformational grammar; we use instead a formal language. This approach is similar to that taken in the formal definition of computer programming languages. In fact, our metalanguage is a modification of the Backus Naur Form (BNF) used in the definition of the programming language Algol (Backus, 1960; Naur, 1960); we refer to it as "modified BNF."

The syntax of transformational grammar, i.e., which strings of symbols are transformational grammars, is defined in modified BNF. The corresponding semantics consists of the algorithms by which a transformational grammar generates sentences; these are specified both by step-by-step descriptions in English and by corresponding computer programs (in the Fortran language).

ADVANTAGES

Using a formal metalanguage to define the form of transformational grammar has several advantages. The definition becomes both precise and concise. Communication between individuals about the form of the grammar is simplified. The process of writing computer programs for grammars is made easier. The form of a grammar can be given a concise statement, convenient for reference. (A complete definition of the form of transformational grammar is included as Appendix B.)

The main purpose of the formal description of grammar is to specify and communicate precisely which sequences of symbols are grammars. Chomsky has stressed from the beginning the importance of defining "rigorously and precisely" the form of a grammar (*Syntactic Structures*, p. 11), and the question of notation for transformational grammar has been much discussed. A formal way of describing proposed notational schemes can make such discussions more meaningful.

Formal descriptions of programming languages are sometimes used directly in syntax-directed translation by computers. We did not design our syntax of transformational grammar for this purpose, and it is unsuitable for it. Instead we intend the syntax for (human) readers.

The modified-BNF metalanguage allows recursive definitions of formats. For example, the syntax rule for *tree* contains the construct *tree* on both sides. As another example, a *structural-analysis* may contain a *term* which is a *choice;* a *choice* is composed of *structural-analyses*. This recursiveness of the syntax brings out the interrelatedness of the parts of a grammar. For example, the

16

prominent role of structural analysis in both lexical insertion and transformation can be seen from the syntax alone. The cross-index to Appendix B shows how the parts of a grammar are related.

A DISADVANTAGE

The disadvantage of a formal metalanguage is that it must be learned by the reader. The rest of this chapter introduces the metalanguage and gives examples of its use. In the initial use of the metalanguage in the text, formal definitions are accompanied by explanations in English. The reader may find it convenient to use this chapter primarily as a reference and to move directly to Chapter 4.

BASIC METALANGUAGE

BNF is simply a formalism for writing a context-free grammar. The BNF description of transformational grammar is a context-free grammar that generates the language consisting of all strings that are transformational grammars. The productions of the BNF grammar are called "syntax rules," to distinguish them from the context-free phrase-structure rules within the transformational grammar. The BNF grammar is referred to as the "syntax" of transformational grammar.

As is the case for programming languages, a BNF description is not quite powerful enough, because the language to be described is not really context-free. Therefore, we supplement some sections of the syntax with constraints in English. The nature of these constraints is explained in the section on limitations of the metalanguage, following the description of the metalanguage.

The following description of modified BNF is illustrated by examples which are actual rules of the syntax. These rules describe only the form of a grammar; the reader can follow the examples without knowing the interpretation of the constructs. Because the syntax rules not only define transformational grammar but also specify the form in which a grammar can be read by the computer program, the constructs are called formats.

PRIMITIVE FORMATS

Basic to the syntax are the two primitive formats *word* and *integer*. A *word* is a contiguous string of upper-case letters and digits beginning with a letter. Examples of *word*s are CHEESECAKE, A111, B, F18T, and NOUN. Examples of strings which are not *word*s are 2ND, AIN'T, 971, GO(O)D, SON-IN-LAW, and D**N. Spaces may not be used in a *word*: the string SNOW PLOW contains two *word*s, the string SNOWPLOW one *word*.

An *integer* is a contiguous string of digits, not beginning with zero. Examples of *integer*s are 1234, 5, 606, and 7000. Examples of strings which are not *integer*s are 0, 09, 8,793, 2.5, and 1 99.

Except in the two formats *integer* and *word*, spaces may be used freely.

BASIC CONVENTIONS[1]

Nonterminal symbols. The nonterminal symbols or format names are the italic hyphenated names of the linguistic constructs.

Examples

> *tree*
>
> *transformational-grammar*

Note that some format names are constructed from more than one English word.

Rewriting symbol. The symbol ::= is the rewriting symbol and is read "is a" or "consists of." For example, the syntax rule

> 4.04   *category-feature* :: = *word*

is read "a category feature is a word." It means that any *word* can be the name of a category feature. An example of a *category-feature* might thus be ADJECTIVE, or even DOG.

Choice. The symbol [] indicates a choice and is read "or." The syntax rule

> 1.02   *node* :: = *word* [] *sentence-symbol* [] *boundary-symbol*

is read "a node is a word or a sentence symbol or a boundary symbol," and it specifies the acceptable types of *nodes*.

Symbols in the language. Symbols which are not in the metalanguage (i.e., symbols other than :: =, [] , [, and]) denote themselves. This includes digits and uppercase letters. For example, the syntax rule

> 1.04   *boundary-symbol* :: = #

asserts that the symbol # is the *boundary-symbol* of the grammar.

Juxtaposition. Juxtaposition in the grammar is indicated by juxtaposition in the metalanguage. Thus, the rule

> 0.01   *transformational-grammar* :: =
>   *phrase-structure lexicon transformations* $

---

[1] The reader familiar with BNF can omit the discussion of basic conventions, noting only that the notation has been modified because the symbols | , ⟨ , and ⟩ are needed in the language itself and so cannot be used in the metalanguage. Angular brackets are replaced by using italic hyphenated names, e.g., *transformational-grammar* rather than ⟨ transformational grammar ⟩, and the symbol | is replaced by [].

says that a *transformational-grammar* consists of *phrase-structure*, immediately followed by *lexicon*, immediately followed by *transformations*, immediately followed by the symbol $.

Another example which illustrates both juxtaposition and the use of symbols to denote themselves is

9.07   *IN-instruction* :: =
        IN *transformation-name* (*integer*) DO ⟨ *control-program* ⟩

Here the symbols IN, (,), DO, ⟨ , and ⟩ denote themselves. If TLOW is a *transformation-name* and Π is a simple *control-program*, the following is an *IN-instruction*: IN TLOW (3) DO ⟨ Π ⟩.

OPERATORS

The syntax rules of the metalanguage describe a linear form for representing a transformational grammar. The definitions are meant for human readers, not for a computer; therefore, we avoid intermediate formats that have no linguistic meaning. To make it possible to have only meaningful formats, we introduce five operators into the metalanguage. These operators are not necessary to the definitions, but they make them simpler. Any occurrence of an operator in a syntax rule could be deleted by the introduction of intermediate formats and corresponding additional rules. This would preserve the form of a grammar, but would change the structure assigned to it.

The five operators are: list, clist, opt, sclist, and booleancombination. They have the interpretations: list, comma list, option, semicolon list, and Boolean combination. The operators are given in lower-case letters; the operand follows within square brackets, as in list[*parameter*] and opt[*integer*].

To illustrate each operator, we give two rules and some possible corresponding strings. The first rule is simple, using the formats *integer* and *word* only; the second is a rule of the syntax for transformational grammar.

The opt operator. Optional elements are indicated by the opt operator; the operand may be included or not included in a corresponding string.

Example 1 The rule

    a ::= opt[*integer*] *word*

allows an *a* to be

    3 POTATOES

or just

    POTATOES

Example 2

2.04   *term* ::=
         opt[*integer*] *structure* [] opt[*integer*] *choice* [] *skip*

If

(V, BEO, WES, WEORTH)

is a *choice,* then both it and

7 (V, BEO, WES, WEORTH)

are *terms.*

The list operator. A list contains items separated only by spaces. It may contain only one item, but must not be empty.

Example 1 The rule

a ::= list[*integer*]

allows an *a* to be any list of *integers,* for example,

1 2 6 9171 3 20

or

91712

Example 2

2.03   *structural-analysis* ::= list[*term*]

If #, %, S 〈 % 1T 〉 , and V are *terms*, then

% S 〈 % 1T 〉 V %

is a *structural-analysis.*

The clist operator. A comma list, called clist ("cee-list"), contains items separated by commas. No comma follows the last item. A clist may contain only one item, but must not be empty.

Example 1 The rule

a ::= clist[*integer*]

allows an *a* to be, for example,

1, 2, 6, 9171, 3, 20

or just

1969

Example 2

2. 07 *choice* ::= (clist[*structural-analysis*])

If V, BEO, WES, and WEORTH are *structural-analyses,* then

(V, BEO, WES, WEORTH)

is a *choice.*

The sclist operator. A semicolon list, called sclist ("ess-cee-list"), is like a clist, but has semicolons in place of commas.

Example 1 **The rule**

a ::= sclist[*integer word*]

allows an *a* to be

3 ROBIN; 2 JAY; 8 FINCH

or

4 SPARROW

It may not be just

WOODPECKER

nor just

515

Example 2

9. 01 *control-program* ::=
       sclist[opt[*label* :] *instruction*]

If TREE and II are *instruction*s then

II; TREE

is a *control-program.* If NEXT is a *label,* then

Γ; NEXT : TREE

is also a *control-program.*

The booleancombination operator. The booleancombination operator indicates that any Boolean combination of instances of its operand can occur in a corresponding string. The logical operators ⌐ (not), & (and) and | (or) are allowed. The precedence order of the operators is: ⌐ is stronger than & is stronger than |. Parentheses may be used to override this precedence order.

Example 1 The rule

a ::= booleancombination[*word*]

allows an *a* to be A & (B | ⌐ D & C) which has the same interpretation as
(A & (B | ((⌐ D) & C))).

Example 2

3.01   *restriction* ::= booleancombination[*condition*]

If 2 EQ 3, 1 DOM ADV, and TRM 2 are *conditions*, then 2 EQ 3 | 1 DOM ADV &
⌐ TRM 4 and (2 EQ 3 | (1 DOM ADV & ⌐ TRM 4)) are *restrictions*, and both
have the same interpretation.

FORMAT NAMES IN THE TEXT

The use of format names has been carried over from the syntax into the text of
this book. When it is important to emphasize that the discussion is about a string
of symbols, rather than about a linguistic concept, the format name is used. For
example, "a complex symbol is a set of feature specifications; a *complex-
symbol* begins with a logical-or (' | ')." In this use, the plural of *trans-
formation* is *transformations*, which is distinct from *transformations*. [2]

COMMENTS IN A GRAMMAR

Two devices permit comments in a grammar. First, expressions within
quotation marks (") are taken to be comments and are not analyzed as part of
the grammar. This makes it possible to insert clarifying remarks at any point.
For example the line

TRANS 1 CP1 "COMPLEMENTIZER PLACEMENT 1".

includes not only the required formal identification of the transformation CP1,
but also some information for readers of the grammar. The glosses of words in
a foreign language can also appear as comments, as in:

GEFAREN "DEAD" AEPEL "NOBEL" LYTEL "LITTLE"

All such comments are ignored by the computer program.

In addition, any *word* which immediately follows the symbol $, with no inter-
vening space, is a comment. This is useful in distinguishing the various uses of
the $ in the grammar. The $ required as the end of *phrase-structure* can be
written $ENDPSG, the one at the end of the *lexicon* $ENDLEX, and so on. In the
computer implementation, the $ that ends the *transformational-grammar* is also
the start of the $MAIN card which controls the computer run.

---

[2] The purist will note that we violate this convention in the case of *structural-
analysis*, using the plural *structural-analyses* in preference to *structural-
analysises*.

LIMITATIONS OF THE METALANGUAGE

The metalanguage chosen is very good for describing the form of individual constructs of a grammar. However, certain requirements on the grammar as a whole cannot be expressed adequately in the metalanguage. The problem is analogous to one that arises in the use of BNF for programming languages. A BNF syntax cannot specify that if a program contains a transfer statement GOTO NEXT, there must be precisely one statement with the label NEXT.

A more general form of this problem occurs in the definition of grammar. For example, *contextual-feature* appears in the syntax rules

    4.06   *contextual-feature* ::= *word*

    7.07   *contextual-definition* ::=
              contextual-feature = *contextual-feature-description*

The *word* COMMON may be used as a *contextual-feature* provided that there is a *contextual-definition* such as

    COMMON = ⟨ NP ⟨ DET _ ⟩⟩

which relates the *word* COMMON to a *contextual-feature-description*. While it is clearly intended that no *word* be used as a *contextual-feature* unless it is so used in a *contextual-definition,* this is not explicitly required by the syntax rules.

Another example is the requirement that no *word* be used in two conflicting ways. For example, no *word* can be both a *contextual-feature* and an *inherent-feature*. Again, a *transformation-name* can be any *word*; but a *control-program* that uses a *transformation-name* that is not in fact the name of a *transformation* is a syntactic violation and results in an uninterpretable instruction in the *control-program.*

Almost all of the other additional conditions on the syntax are likewise necessary to make a grammar meaningful. Even without knowing the conditions, a user would not be likely to violate any of them intentionally, because the resulting grammar would not make sense. The computer program, however, does carry out extensive error checking, and will complain about violations.

The decision to use a metalanguage that is not quite powerful enough and requires occasional supplementation is a compromise which we believe is justified by the resulting simplicity of the BNF description and by the infrequency of qualifying remarks.

In addition to the cases where the formal syntax must unavoidably be augmented by qualifying clauses, some rules have deliberately been written so that qualification is necessary. Where the choice is between a simple qualification and the introduction of several intermediate formats, clarity is best served by the use of a constraint. An example is the definition of *element:*

    2.06   *element* ::= *node* [] * [] _

For *transformations,* this definition of *element* must be modified to exclude the underline ; for *contextual-feature-descriptions* the first *element* may not be either * or _ , although other *elements* may be of any of the three types. This distinction could easily be expressed by adding more syntax rules, but to do so would obscure an important similarity between transformations and contextual features.

## CHAPTER 4

Trees

In this chapter the formal presentation of the model begins. The overall goal is to explicate the format *transformational-grammar*. To do this it is necessary to show how each part of that format is in turn constructed from other formats, until finally the definition is reducible to symbols and primitive formats.

The first syntax rule defines the format *transformational-grammar*:

> 0. 01   *transformational-grammar* ::=
>   *phrase-structure lexicon transformations* $

That is, a *transformational-grammar* consists of *phrase-structure*, followed by *lexicon*, followed by *transformations*, followed by the symbol $. The number 0. 01 indicates the position of this rule in the full syntax. The explanation of the three formats on the right in rule 0. 01 first requires some basic concepts. The format *phrase-structure* and the phrase structure component of a grammar are the first major goal; to reach it, the basic concept of a tree must first be considered.

TREES

The notion of tree is basic to transformational grammar; in one sense, a grammar is simply a device for generating and modifying trees. The computer model includes two forms for trees, a linear form and a tabular form. The linear form, defined in the formal metalanguage, is used for trees that appear as subparts of a grammar, and can also serve for input of trees. The alternative tabular form, which is easier to read for large trees, is used for output and optionally for input.

In this book, we generally use the customary tree diagrams in informal discussion. Occasionally, in presenting examples that have been worked out on the computer, we use the tabular tree form.

The terminology to be used in discussing trees is next introduced. Then the formats for the linear forms *tree* and *tree-specification* are defined. Finally, the alternative tabular tree form is presented.

TERMINOLOGY

There will be frequent occasions to refer to the relationships among the nodes of a tree. The terms given here are used throughout the book. The definitions are almost the usual ones; an exception is made with respect to the sentence symbol in the definition of dominance.

A simple example of a tree is

(1)

The *root*, here the sentence symbol S, is the node at the top. A node X is a *daughter* of node Y if X is immediately below Y and connected to Y. In the example, N is a daughter of NP, VP is a daughter of S. If X is a daughter of Y, then Y is the *parent* of X. We say also that X is *immediately dominated* by Y. In the example, NP is the parent of both DET and N; V is immediately dominated by VP.

X *dominates* Y if X is above Y and connected to Y by a chain not containing an internal occurrence of the sentence symbol S. Without the restriction on sentence symbols, the definition would be that X dominates Y if there is a chain $X = X_0, X_1, \ldots, X_n = Y$ such that X_i immediately dominates X_{i+1} for $0 \leq i < n$. This implies that a node does not dominate itself. The definition is modified so that the chain must not include an S except at the ends; that is, $X_i \neq S$ for $0 < i < n$. In tree (2), node 3 dominates node 7 even though 7 is an S, but node 3 does not dominate node 8 because node 7 is an internal S in the chain connecting 3 and 8.

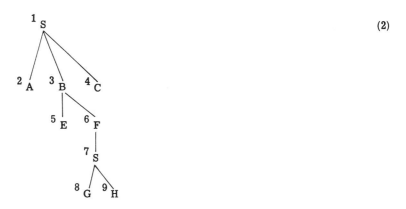

(2)

X *is dominated by* Y if Y dominates X. The exclusion of internal sentence symbols in these definitions is natural for transformational grammar, and is assumed throughout unless explicit exception is made.

X is a *sister* of Y if X and Y have the same parent. One sister is distinguished as *the* right (left) sister. X is *the right (left) sister* of Y, if X is a sister of Y and is to the immediate right (left) of Y in the left-to-right list of daughters of the common parent. This distinction is important in adding nodes to trees because sister adjunction adjoins a node as the (immediate) right or left sister of another node.

The *subtree* headed by X consists of X and all tree structure beneath X and connected to X. No special case is made here for nodes S.

Example: In tree (2) node 1, S, is the root. Nodes 2, 3, and 4 are the daughters of node 1. Node 1 immediately dominates nodes 2, 3, and 4, dominates 2, 3, 4, 5, 6, and 7, but does not dominate 8 or 9. Nodes 3 and 4 are sisters of 2; node 3 is the right sister of node 2.

THE FORMAT

By using angular brackets to indicate changes of level, tree (1) can be written in linear form:

S ⟨ NP ⟨ DET N ⟩ VP ⟨ V ⟩ ⟩

The daughters of a node now appear to the right of the node, and are surrounded by angular brackets.

This linear form for trees is formally described by four syntax rules. (Rule 1.01' is a simplified version of rule 1.01, given later.)

   1.01'   *tree* ::= *node* opt[⟨ list[*tree*] ⟩]

   1.02   *node* ::= *word* ⫿ *sentence-symbol* ⫿ *boundary-symbol*

   1.03   *sentence-symbol* ::= S

   1.04   *boundary-symbol* ::= #

The optional list of *tree*s within angular brackets in a *tree* is the list of daughter subtrees of the preceding node. This list is in left to right order. The daughters of X are within the pair of brackets immediately following X and not within any other pair of brackets not containing X.

The symbol S is distinguished by its appearance in rule 1.03. It may only be used as the *sentence-symbol* and may not be used as a *word*. A consequence of this is that sentence symbols in other languages may require change; for example, the French "P" for "proposition" must be translated to English "S". Also, caution must be used in selecting a *word* to represent the plural morpheme "S".

The *boundary-symbol* is the only special (non-alphanumeric) character which may appear as a *node* in a *tree*.

Complex symbols

Complex symbols will not be properly introduced until Chapter 6. Nonetheless, in order to complete the discussion of trees, the position of *complex-symbols* in a *tree* is treated here. The reader may wish to return to this section.

In a *tree*, a *complex-symbol* may optionally follow any *node*, and precedes the list of subtrees of that *node*. The full syntax rule for *tree* is thus:

1. 01   *tree* ::=   *node* opt[*complex-symbol*] opt[⟨list[*tree*] ⟩]

A *complex-symbol* is delimited by vertical bars, rather than by the large square brackets used in figures. Consider, for example, the tree

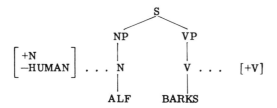

Without the complex symbols this would be

S ⟨ NP ⟨ N ⟨ ALF ⟩⟩ VP ⟨ V ⟨ BARKS ⟩⟩⟩

With the complex symbols it is

S ⟨ NP ⟨ N | +N −HUMAN |⟨ ALF ⟩⟩ VP ⟨ V | +V |⟨ BARKS ⟩⟩⟩

An extended example of a *tree* is

S ⟨ # NP ⟨ N | +N +HUMAN |⟨ GEORGE ⟩⟩ VP ⟨ V | +V ⌋
⟨ SAW ⟩ NP ⟨ DET | +DET |⟨ THE ⟩ N | +N −ANIMATE −ABSTRACT |
⟨ MOVIE ⟩⟩⟩ # ⟩

Tree specification

The linear form of a large tree can be quite cumbersome and unreadable. One way of alleviating this problem is to give the tree in several parts, which are combined in a well-defined way. A substitution facility, defined by the format *tree-specification*, is provided for that purpose. The syntax is given by the rule:

tree-specification ::=   *tree* opt[, clist[*word tree*]].

An example of a *tree-specification* is

S ⟨ A B ⟨ E DUMMY ⟩ C ⟩ , DUMMY F ⟨ S ⟨ G H ⟩⟩ .

The *tree* preceding the first comma contains a dummy node, in this case DUMMY. The optional part contains a one-member clist, containing the *word* DUMMY and the *tree* F ⟨ S ⟨ G H ⟩ ⟩. This *tree* is substituted for the node DUMMY in the initial tree, with the result

S ⟨ A B ⟨ E F ⟨ S ⟨ G H ⟩⟩⟩ C ⟩

This is tree (2), illustrated earlier.

More generally, the *word tree* pairs in the clist are processed from left to right. A pair *word*$_i$ *tree*$_i$ is interpreted to mean that the (unique) occurrence of *word*$_i$ in the tree so far constructed is to be replaced by the subtree *tree*$_i$.

A *tree-specification* may be used as the input form for a tree. A *tree* followed by a period is a simple *tree-specification.*

TABULAR FORM

The second type of tree representation in the model is a tabular form, which is used for all output of the computer system and may also be used for input. The input or output medium is divided into "fields" of equal width. For input the fields are six columns wide; for output they are twelve columns wide. The tabular tree begins with a first line or card which contains an identifying title for the tree. This title is never processed by the program. The tree is terminated by a blank card on input; on output, it ends with the string of terminal symbols of the tree.

In the tabular input form, tree (1) would appear as

TREE (1)

S	NP	DET
		N
	VP	V

(blank)

This form is essentially a mirror reflection of the tree, followed by a deformation which puts the leftmost daughter of a node on the same line and in the field immediately to the right of the node. Daughters to the right appear below the leftmost daughter. Informally, the directions "right" and "below" have been interchanged. The reader may find it helpful at first to draw in the lines connecting a node and its daughters, as in

TREE (1)

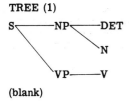

(blank)

A slightly more complicated example is

TREE TYPE FOR "THE MONGOOSE BIT JOHN"

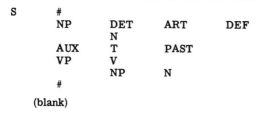

```
S      #
       NP       DET      ART      DEF
                N
       AUX      T        PAST
       VP       V
                NP       N
       #

       (blank)
```

This represents the tree

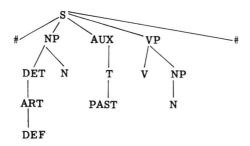

On output, a number appears with each node. These node numbers correspond to the order in which the nodes were read in, generated by the phrase structure component, or added by transformations. If tree (1) is read in, and then printed out without further processing, the result is:

TREE (1)

1 S	2 NP	3 DET
		4 N
	5 VP	6 V

DET N V

Substitution feature

A potential difficulty in the tabular format is that the depth of a tree may exceed the maximum number of fields. The substitution feature avoids this, replacing subtrees by dummy nodes. Substitution is indicated by the use of a line with the distinguished string XXX in the first field and the arbitrary dummy node in the second. Thus,

A TREE WITH SUBSTITUTION

S	B	C
	D	E	F
		DUM
	H	
XXX	DUM	
S	B	C
	D	
	(blank)	

represents the tree

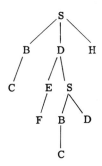

The only restriction on the use of the substitution feature on input is that a unique name be given to the dummy node for which the subtree is to be substituted. A substitution is made only for the first occurrence of a name.

The subtree need not have the sentence symbol as root, although on output the sentence symbol is generally used.

Complex symbols

Complex symbols do not fit conveniently into the tabular tree form, and must be given following the tree. The exact pattern is different on input and output.

On input a substitution line with **XXX** and a dummy node is used with CS in field three to signal that a node with complex symbol follows instead of a tree. In the following example, the node SUB3 is replaced by a subtree, and node N1 and node N2 are each replaced by a node N with complex symbol | +**SG** − **PRO** |.

SENTENCE TYPE 35

S	#			
	NP	DET	ART	INDEF
			SUB3	
		N1	BOY	
	AUX	T	PAST	
	VP	V		
	#			
XXX	SUB3			
S	#			
	NP	DET	ART	WH
				INDEF
		N2	BOY	
	AUX	T	PRES	
	VP	BE		
		ADJ		
	#			
XXX	N1	CS		
N | +SG	—PRO |			
XXX	N2	CS		
N | +SG	—PRO |			
		(blank)		

On output, complex symbols are printed between the tree and the terminal string; node numbers indicate their positions, as in the following example. (The internal structure of complex symbols is explained later.)

```
DOES IT WORK?
   1 S           2 #
                 3 C
                 4 NP      1C N       13 HE
                 5 AUX     15 C
                 6 VP       8 VB      12 SHAKE
                           9 NP      11 N        14 SHE
                 7 #
NODE  1C N
         |+N +SINC +FRC +MASC +III −ACC|
NODE   5 AUX
         |+AUX −MCC +PAST|
NOCE   8 VB
         |+VB +UP +PRT +FRCC +FERF +<VF<_NP>>|
NOCE  11 N
         |+N +SINC +FRC +FEM +III −ACC|

         #Q HE C SHAKE SHE#
```

## CHAPTER 5

The Phrase Structure Component

The first component of a *transformational-grammar* is *phrase-structure*. The phrase structure grammar is an ordered context-free grammar. The algorithm associated with the phrase structure component is tree generation. We first describe the format *phrase-structure*, then define derivation relative to a phrase structure grammar, and finally present the component algorithm of the model. This algorithm is a method of directed random generation of trees that allows the user to specify beforehand some of the characteristics of the output tree. The algorithm generates a tree that meets the specifications and is otherwise random.

THE FORMAT

The usual linguistic representation of a phrase structure grammar is nonlinear. A typical rule might be

$$
VP \rightarrow \left\{ \begin{array}{c} AUX \left\{ \begin{array}{l} MV \quad (NP) \\ \\ COP \left(\left\{ \begin{array}{l} NP \\ AP \end{array} \right\} \right) \end{array} \right\} \quad (ADV) \\ \\ S \end{array} \right\}
$$

The format allows a compact linear representation of this rule as:

VP = (AUX (MV (NP), COP ((NP, AP))), S) (ADV).

In the linear form braces have been replaced by parentheses, and items which would be displayed on different lines within braces are now separated by commas. The resulting use of parentheses for both option and choice is not ambiguous, because parentheses around a single item indicate optionality, e.g.,

---

Partial descriptions of the system appeared earlier in two papers in the *Communications of the ACM*, **12** (1969), 40-46 and 341-348. The ACM has granted permission for use of the figures from those papers.

(ADV) in the VP rule above, and parentheses around two or more items separated by commas indicate choice, e.g., (NP, AP). An optional choice is specified by a double set of parentheses, e.g., ((NP, AP)).

The syntactic definition of *phrase-structure* is:

6.01   *phrase-structure ::=*
          PHRASESTRUCTURE list [*phrase-structure-rule*] $
6.02   *phrase-structure-rule ::= rule-left = rule-right.*
6.03   *rule-left ::= node*
6.04   *rule-right ::= node* [] list[*rule-right*] [] (clist[*rule-right*])

Example[1]

```
         "IBM CORE GRAMMAR"
PHRASESTRUCTURE
S   = # ( PRE ) NP AUX VP # .
PRE = ( NEG ) ( Q ) .
AUX = T ( M ) .
T   = ( PRES, PAST ) .
VP  = ( HAVE EN ) ( BE ING ) ( V ( ( NP, PP ) ) ( ( S, PP ) ) ( MAN ) , BE
        ( ADJ ) ) .
PP  = PREP NP .
MAN = PREP P .
NP  = ( DET ) N ( S ) .
DET = ART ( S ) .
ART = ( WH ) ( DEF, INDEF ) .
          $ END
```

Expansion of rules

For the process of sentence generation it is convenient to have the right-hand side of each rule expressed as a choice of strings, none of which itself contains options or choices. Expanding the *rule-right* by removing options and choices produces an equivalent *expanded-rule-right*:

   expanded-rule-right ::= clist[list [*node*]]

The lists of *node*s in the *expanded-rule-right* are referred to as the "expansions" of the *rule-left*.

The set of expansions of a node is understood not to include the null expansion. If the conventions produce the null expansion, it is discarded. Thus, the rule, ASP = (PERF) (PROG)., gives ASP the three expansions PROG, PERF PROG, and PERF. Redundant parentheses are allowed but have no meaning. For example, MV((NP)) is equivalent to MV(NP), and COP(((NP, AP))) is equivalent to COP((NP, AP)).

The computer program expands the *phrase-structure-rule*s as it reads in the grammar. Figure 10 shows a *phrase-structure* and its expanded form.

---

[1] Throughout the book we use as examples parts of grammars which have been run on the computer. We make no claim for linguistic validity; they are simply examples of notation.

As input:

    "VERSION OF UCLAG 15 SEPT 67"
    PHRASESTRUCTURE
S = # (S CONJ S (CONJ S), (PRE) NP VP (ADV)) # .
VP = (AUX (MV (NP), COP ((NP, AP))), S) (ADV).
MV = V (ADV).
AP = ADJ.
AUX = TNS (M (IMP)) (ASP).
ADV = (PREP NP, ADVB).
NP = D (NOM, S).
NOM = ((NOM) S, N).
D = ART (POST).
PRE = NEG.
CONJ = ((WH) OR, BUT, AND).
ASP = (PERF) (PROG).
POST = QUANT.
IMP = (NOT) (PLEASE) IMPER.
$END

Expanded form produced by input routine:

1	S =	33	ADV =
2	# S CONJ S CONJ S # ,	34	PREP NP,
3	# S CONJ S # ,	35	ADVB.
4	# PRE NP VP ADV # ,	36	NP =
5	# PRE NP VP # ,	37	D S,
6	# NP VP ADV # ,	38	D NOM.
7	# NP VP # .	39	NOM =
8	VP =	40	S,
9	S ADV,	41	NOM S,
10	S,	42	N.
11	AUX MV NP ADV,	43	D =
12	AUX MV NP,	44	ART POST,
13	AUX MV ADV,	45	ART.
14	AUX MV,	46	PRE =
15	AUX COP NP ADV,	47	NEG.
16	AUX COP NP,	48	CONJ =
17	AUX COP AP ADV,	49	WH OR,
18	AUX COP AP,	50	OR,
19	AUX COP ADV,	51	BUT,
20	AUX COP.	52	AND.
21	MV =	53	ASP =
22	V ADV,	54	PROG,
23	V.	55	PERF PROG,
24	AP =	56	PERF.
25	ADJ.	57	POST =
26	AUX =	58	QUANT.
27	TNS M IMP ASP,	59	IMP =
28	TNS M IMP,	60	PLEASE IMPER,
29	TNS M ASP,	61	NOT PLEASE IMPER,
30	TNS M,	62	NOT IMPER,
31	TNS ASP,	63	IMPER.
32	TNS.		

Figure 10. Phrase-structure

Ordering conditions

Some requirements on the *phrase-structure* cannot be readily formalized in modified-BNF. These requirements stem from the fact that the phrase-structure algorithm assumes that the rules are ordered. Specifically, the conditions are:

(i)   The *rule-left* of the first *phrase-structure-rule* must be the *sentence-symbol*. This condition enters because the algorithm begins with the root of the tree and the first rule.

(ii)   Except for the *sentence-symbol*, no *node* is reintroduced after the rule that expands it. However, a *node* may occur in both the *rule-left* and the *rule-right* of a single rule. Chomsky suggests in *Aspects* (p. 137) that recursiveness in the phrase structure component is limited to reintroduction of the sentence symbol. Our constraint is less restrictive, since it allows other recursion, for example, NOM = ((NOM) S, N) .

It does not, however, allow loops such as

NOMP = (NOM, NOM CONJ NOM) .

NOM   = ((INTENS) (DP) NP, # S #) .

NP   = (NOMP) (# S #) N .

(iii) No *node* may occur as *rule-left* in more than one rule. The algorithm uses the first applicable rule. If a *node* were to appear as *rule-left* in two rules, one of them would never apply, since by (ii) no *node* is reintroduced after expansion.

The computer implementation imposes requirements (ii) and (iii) only if the DOM and NDOM constraints of the generation routine are used (see p. 44). Otherwise, they can be weakened to:

(iv) Each *node* that occurs as *rule-left* at all occurs as *rule-left* of one rule after the last rule in which it occurs in the *rule-right*. For example, the following grammar is permitted ,under this weak requirement:

"AFESP CASE GRAMMAR I"

```
PHRASESTRUCTURE
        S = # AUX VP # .
        VP = V ( NPO ) ( NPD ) ( NPL ) ( NPI ) ( NPA ) .
        NPA = A NP .
        NPI = I NP .
        NPD = D NP .
        NPL = L NP .
        NPO = O NP .
        NP = DET NOM .
        NOM = N ( NPO ) ( NPD ) ( NPL ) ( NPA ) .
        NPA = A NP .
        NPD = D NP .
        NPL = L NP .
        NPO = O NP .
        NP = DET NOM .
        NOM = N .
         $ENDPSG
```

This grammar approximates an unordered grammar with recursion on symbols other than S, but does not generate arbitrarily deep structures. This is an advantage in actual generation.

Remarks on the syntax

The decision to use context-free rather than context-sensitive rules follows the treatment in *Aspects* and the current trend in the literature. The use of a context-sensitive grammar would have introduced no problems except in the random generation algorithm, where it would complicate the treatment of the constraints, particularly the equality constraint.

It may be noted that the syntax rules do not restrict the use of the boundary symbol. The linguist would presumably wish to use the boundary symbol only as a terminal, and to introduce it in appropriate pairs.

Rule schemata

The model does not contain any provision for rule schemata, which abbreviate infinite sets of expansions. Rule schemata are usually expressed with the Kleene star, as in:

S = (ADV*) NOMP PREDP AUX.

This schema introduces ADV zero or more times. The resulting expansions of S are thus NOMP PREDP AUX, ADV NOMP PREDP AUX, ADV ADV NOMP PREDP AUX, and so on ad infinitum.

Although the model does not allow such a schema, the computer program can nonetheless be used to explore its effect. Any finite number of expansions can be introduced in a single rule. For the previous schema, it would probably suffice to allow, say, up to four ADV, which could be done by the rule:

S = (ADV) (ADV) (ADV) (ADV) NOMP PREDP AUX.

An apparent alternative to this construction would be introduce a new symbol ADVN with the two rules

S   = (ADVN) NOMP PREDP AUX .
ADVN = ADV (ADVN) .

However, this is not equivalent because it does not preserve structure.

THE GENERATION PROBLEM

One valuable way to provide feedback to the grammar writer is by exercising the grammar as a generator. If the phrase structure component produces interesting base trees, they can serve as inputs to the lexical and transformational components. However, purely random base trees are unsatisfactory for several reasons. If the phrase structure rules are recursive, the derivation may fail to terminate. An even more serious problem is that the relation between embedding and embedded subtrees is special in transformational grammar, so that almost any tree generated at random blocks in the transformation phase.[2]

Even if these difficulties could be somehow bypassed, the linguist needs some control over the generator. At any given time some types of trees are more interesting to him than others; he may wish to test some particular set of transformations, or to study trees with a particular subtree, and so on. It is desirable both to constrain the generation away from the pitfalls of infinite length and blocking and to direct it toward areas of interest.

The solution offered here is a directed random generator, which is as random as you like, but not more so. The user gives a rough description of the tree desired, and the algorithm then generates a tree meeting the description, but otherwise using phrase structure expansions selected at random. If the algorithm begins with a sentence symbol only, then the result is a random tree without embedding. In the more general case, the algorithm starts with an input in the form of a tree, called a "skeleton," which it is to fill out. The skeleton may contain several types of indicators of the type of tree desired as the final result. If these instructions do not conflict with the phrase structure grammar, they are followed.

The use of a skeleton to direct the generation process is the novel and distinguishing feature of the phrase structure generation algorithm in the model. The scheme was designed to make it possible to generate trees which are "interesting" rather than simply random—in particular, to generate trees which will test specific transformations. Users occasionally need several tries to find the right skeleton to test a particular transformation. Once found, however, a skeleton continues to be used even after other transformations of the grammar are modified.

The process of constrained or directed random generation is a modification of the normal generation process. It is easier to explain the standard algorithm first, then the modified process.

RANDOM GENERATION

We describe the algorithm, then give an example. At any point in a derivation some rule of the phrase structure is the current rule. There is a current tree and its terminal string is the current string. The current string is actually two strings: parallel to the string of symbols is a string of corresponding node numbers in the tree. In the simplest case the derivation begins with a tree which consists of one node, S, and its corresponding terminal string, which also consists only of S. The first rule of the grammar is initially the current rule.

The current string is scanned to find the leftmost occurrence of the current *rule-left*. If there is none, the next rule becomes the current rule and the scan

---

[2] Klima (1965) suggests an alternative solution to this problem. Basically Klima's proposal is that lexical insertion in the currently lowest sentence be alternated with transformation and embedding of the lowest sentence, allowing agreements between embedding and embedded sentences to be forced by the structural change of the embedding transformation. The feasibility of this idea could be explored by minor modifications to this computer system.

is repeated. (Here we take advantage of the requirement that the phrase structure rules be ordered.) If an occurrence of the current *rule-left* is found, an expansion is picked at random[3] from the *expanded-rule-right* of the current rule. The nodes of the expansion are attached as daughters of the tree node. The string node is replaced by the nodes of the expansion. The process now repeats from the beginning of this paragraph.

When the current rule is the last rule, and no more occurrences of its *rule-left* are found, the derivation terminates unless there are sentence symbols in the current string. In that case, the rules must be recycled. First, however, the string is reduced to a string of sentence symbols only, by deleting all occurrences of other symbols. The first rule then becomes the current rule and the process is repeated.

We illustrate the process using a simplified phrase structure grammar for Japanese.

> "JAPANESE SYNTAX"
>
> PHRASESTRUCTURE
>
> "1"   S = # NP (NP) (NP) V T # .
>
> "2"   NP = (S) N .
>
> "3"   T = (PRES, PAST) .
>
> $ ENDPSG

Initially, the tree has only a sentence symbol. This symbol is also the only symbol in the string.

> Current tree: 1 S
>
> Current string: Node number: 1
>   Symbol: S

The current rule is rule 1, which has rule-left S.

The string is searched for the leftmost occurrence of S. The symbol found corresponds to node 1 of the tree. An expansion for S is picked at random from the three possible expansions given by rule 1. Suppose that the expansion # NP NP V T # is chosen. The tree and string are now modified yielding:

> Current tree: 1 S   2 #
>   3 NP
>   4 NP
>   5 V
>   6 T
>   7 #
>
> Current string: Node number: 2   3   4   5   6   7
>   Symbol: #   NP   NP   V   T   #

---

[3] The phrase "at random" means according to a uniform probability distribution. Each object in the space has an equal chance of being selected.

Rule 1 is still the current rule. The string is scanned for an occurrence of S, but since none is found rule 2 becomes the current rule.

The rule-left is now NP and the second symbol in the string is the leftmost NP. An expansion is chosen at random; suppose S N is selected. The results are:

Current tree: 1 S   2 #
                    3 NP   8 S
                              9 N
                    4 NP
                    5 V
                    6 T
                    7 #

Current string:	Node number:	2	8	9	4	5	6	7
	Symbol:	#	S	N	NP	V	T	#

Rule 2 is still current so the string is again searched from left-to-right for an NP. Node 4 is found. This time the expansion N is selected at random, with the results:

Current tree: 1 S   2 #
                    3 NP   8 S
                              9 N
                    4 NP   10 N
                    5 V
                    6 T
                    7 #

Current string:	Node number:	2	8	9	10	5	6	7
	Symbol:	#	S	N	N	V	T	#

One more step, and a random choice of PAST as the expansion of T, gives:

Current tree: 1 S   2 #
                    3 NP   8 S
                              9 N
                    4 NP   10 N
                    5 V
                    6 T   11 PAST
                    7 #

Current string:	Node number:	2	8	9	10	5	11	7
	Symbol:	#	S	N	N	V	PAST	#

The current rule is now the last rule and there are no more occurrences of T in the string. The string is now reduced to:

Current string:	Node number:	8
	Symbol:	S

The current rule is again the first rule, and the process is repeated. (The point of removing nodes #, N, V, PAST, and # from the string is that in an ordered grammar, a symbol (other than S) may be expanded only in the same cycle in which it is introduced.)

The process is repeated until the last rule is the current rule, its rule-left does not occur in the string, and there are no more sentence symbols in the string. A possible result for this sample derivation is:

```
1 S    2 #                                                    (1)
       3 NP     8 S        12 #
                           13 NP    17 N
                           14 V
                           15 T     18 PRES
                           16 #

                9 N
       4 NP    10 N
       5 V
       6 T     11 PAST
       7 #
      ## N V PRES # N N V PAST #
```

After lexical insertion and transformation the generated sentence might be:

FURUI TOMODACHI GA SUKIYAKI O TABETA— "An old friend ate sukiyaki"

BASIC SKELETONS

The user can direct the generation algorithm by three different means. He can give a basic skeleton which will be part of the final tree. He can put constraints on the basic skeleton to control the subtrees to which certain nodes may be expanded. Finally, he can add node variables to the basic skeleton to further direct the generation at certain points. We discuss each of these devices in detail.

A basic skeleton must satisfy two conditions. (1) A final tree can be gotten from it by adding lines and nodes (without altering the existing ones). (2) If a node has daughters in the basic skeleton, no new daughters need be added between them. This definition can be stated more formally, using two preliminary definitions.

A subgraph of a tree T is a tree T_0 which can be obtained from T by deleting 0 or more nodes and all lines connected to those nodes. For example,

is a subgraph of

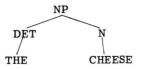

but

is not

A subgraph T_0 of a tree T is *adjacency-preserving* if adjacent daughters of every node in T_0 are also adjacent in T. For example, both

and

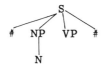

are subgraphs of

but only the first one is adjacency-preserving.

A *basic skeleton* (for a phrase structure grammar G) is an adjacency-preserving subgraph of some tree of G.

Suppose that a directed random generation begins with the basic skeleton T_0 and results in the tree T. Then T has the same root as T_0, and contains T_0 as an adjacency-preserving subgraph. (It follows that the root of the main skeleton must be the sentence symbol.)

Examples. Two basic skeletons for the Japanese phrase structure grammar on p. 38 are:

(2)

(3)

Tree (1) is a possible result of a directed generation from either (2) or (3).
Tree (4) is a possible result of (3) but not of (2).

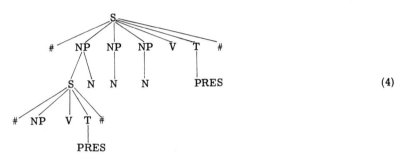

(4)

Two trees which are not basic skeletons for Japanese are:

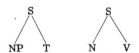

CONSTRAINTS

Some goals for the generation process cannot easily be expressed by a basic
skeleton. For example, to use a basic skeleton to specify that a tree must not
contain an ADV it would be necessary to include the expansions of all nodes
which could otherwise immediately dominate ADV. To require that two NP s
be equal, it would be necessary to include both of their subtrees in full in the
basic skeleton. The use of constraints is an easier way to express such
conditions.

Three types of contraints are provided: dominance, nondominance, and equality.
We first discuss the representation of constraints, then define each type and
illustrate its use.

Representation

A constraint is attached to a basic skeleton as three consecutive daughters of
the node to which it applies. The dominance, nondominance, and equality

contraints have the forms RES DOM *node,* RES NDOM *node,* and RES EQ *integer.*[4]

General form:

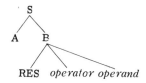

Example:

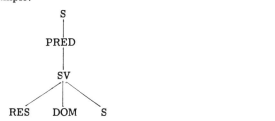

(5)

The same example in tabular form:

SKELETON FOR ONE EMBEDDING

S	PRED	SV	RES
			DOM
			S

A basic skeleton to which constraints and special variables have been added is called a *restricted skeleton* or sometimes just *skeleton.*

Dominance constraint

If a node A bears the constraint RES DOM B, then, in the resulting tree, node A will dominate at least one node B. Since no sentence symbols are introduced unless specified in the skeleton, RES DOM S is often used to generate embedded sentences, as in (5).

The operand of the dominance constraint need not be just a node, but may be a restricted skeleton. Examples (6) and (7) show constraints below dominance constraints. In (6) the embedded S dominates an N which is constrained to be equal to another N. Example (7) also illustrates the use of two constraints on a single node. The constraints RES NDOM PV and RES DOM S both apply to the same node S. The S introduced by the dominance constraint must also not dominate PV.

---

[4] Constraints were originally called "restrictions." The name was changed to avoid confusion with the related but different restrictions that appear in structural descriptions of transformations. The mnemonic RES remains.

```
        V4 WITH REL CLAUSE
S       #
        NP      S       RES
                        DOM
                        N       RES
                                EQ
                                1

                N       RES                                        (6)
                        EQ
                        1
        NP
        V
        T       PRES
        #
```

```
        NEGATIVE PERFORMATIVE
S       #
        NP      N       BOKU
        S       RES
                NDOM
                PV
                RES                                                (7)
                DOM
                S       RES
                        NDOM
                        PV
        PV
        #
```

Nondominance constraint

If a node A bears the constraint RES NDOM B, then, in the final tree, node A does not dominate any B. Thus, (8) specifies that the lowest S does not dominate any node PV. In (7) the constraint RES NDOM PV is given twice, for two S's, one of which dominates the other. Both occurrences of the constraint are necessary, because nondominance constraints do not go beyond embedded S's. (This follows from the definition of dominance given in Chapter 4.)

```
        SENTENTIAL WITH EMBEDDED V3
S       #
        S       #
                NP
                S       RES
                        NDOM
                        PV
                V
                T       PRES                                       (8)
                #
        V
        T       PRES
        #
```

An important use of the nondominance constraint is to avoid the lengthy trees which would otherwise be generated by recursive phrase structure rules such as NP = NP AND NP.

Equality constraint

The equality constraint forces two or more nodes to have identical subtrees. For any integer i, all nodes with the constraint RES EQ i will dominate identical subtrees. (The choice of i is arbitrary; it simply relates equality constraints to one another.) The algorithm actually expands only the first node it encounters for a particular i and copies the result to the other nodes constrained by RES EQ i. As a consequence of this method, only this first node may have a partial expansion or have additional constraints.

The equality constraint makes it possible to generate base trees for relative sentences and other embeddings which require equality. Example (6) is the basis for a sentence with a relative clause.

Figure 11 shows both a skeleton with equality constraints and a tree generated from that skeleton using the grammar of Figure 10.

NODE VARIABLES

The third device for allowing the user to direct sentence generation is the node variable. The three symbols X, Y, and NL (null) are used as node variables. Each conveys an instruction to the generation algorithm about the expansion of its parent node:

X: Insert 0 or more nodes at this point

Y: Insert 1 or more nodes at this point

NL: Insert nothing at this point

Node variables X and Y, inserted between daughters of a node, vitiate the adjacency condition and thus change the set of possible trees (see Figure 12a). The variable Y also has meaning when used as a first or last daughter, although an X in that position is redundant. Because of the adjacency condition, NL is meaningful only as the leftmost or rightmost daughter; it prevents expansion in that direction. (See Figure 12b.)

LIMITATION ON INTRODUCTION OF S

The random generation algorithm never introduces a sentence symbol unless it is given in the basic skeleton or specified by a constraint. The result (1) is not produced from a sentence symbol only, as in the example, because the algorithm does not select the expansion S N for NP unless directed to do so. From a single S, it generates only sentences not containing any other S. Skeletons (2) and (3) lead to final trees containing precisely two S's. Any desired amount of embedding can be obtained from suitable skeletons.

This restriction on the generation algorithm was made for two reasons. First, if base trees with internal sentence symbols are generated at random, they almost uniformly fail during the transformational phase of the generation. Second, the restriction tends to keep the size of the generated tree within reasonable limits.

Skeleton as input

```
S       NP      RES
                EQ
                1
        VP      S       NP
                        VP      AUX
                                MV
                                NP      RES
                                        EQ
                                        1
```

Generated tree (Node numbers reflect the order of generation.)

```
1 S   16 #
      17 PRE    31 NEG
      2 NP      22 D      28 ART
                23 NOM    26 N
      6 VP      7 S       33 #
                          8 NP      44 D      50 ART
                                              51 POST    54 QUANT
                                    45 NOM    48 N
                          9 VP      10 AUX    38 TNS
                                              39 M
                                              40 ASP     53 PROG
                                    11 MV     37 V
                                    55 NP     56 D       58 ART
                                              57 NOM     59 N
                                    36 ADV    41 PREP
                                              42 NP      46 D      52 ART
                                                         47 NOM    49 N
                          34 ADV    43 ADVB
                          35 #
      18 ADV    20 PREP
                21 NP     24 D      29 ART
                                    30 POST    32 QUANT
                          25 NOM    27 N
      19 #
#      NEG ART N    # ART QUANT N   TNS M     PROG V ART N
PREP ART N ADVB #   PREP ART QUANT N #
```

Figure 11. A skeleton and an output tree

Rule: S = # (S CONJ S(CONJ S), (PRE) NP VP) #

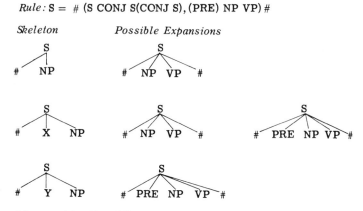

(a) Variables **X** and **Y**

Rule: VP = (AUX(MV (NP), COP((NP, AP))), S) (ADV).

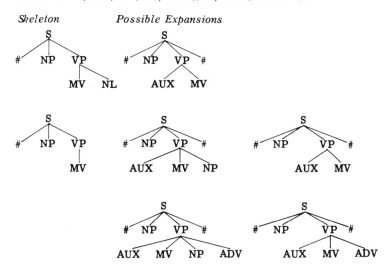

(b) Null variable, NL·

Figure 12.   Use of node variables

COMBINATIONS OF CONDITIONS

The only limitation on the combined use of basic skeletons, constraints, and node variables is that a NDOM constraint may not be further modified. For example, the node introduced by a dominance constraint may, in turn, be the root of a skeleton, as in

```
S       RES
        DOM
        NP      N
                S
```

The result will contain an NP dominating adjacent N S.

The skeleton may contain vocabulary words, provided that their lexical category is given. The skeleton below expands to a sentence containing "HAMMER."

```
S       RES
        DOM
        N           HAMMER
```

Complex symbols may likewise be given as part of the skeleton, but there is generally little reason to do so, because they are added automatically. The treatment of these cases is discussed in the chapter on lexical insertion.

THE GENERATION ALGORITHM

We describe the generation of a tree about a skeleton in terms of the differences from the basic generation algorithm given on p. 37. Figure 13 is an illustration of the process; it uses the grammar of Figure 10.

When the derivation begins, the skeleton is the current tree, and the root of the skeleton, which must be a sentence symbol, is the current string. At each step the node to be expanded is selected from the string exactly as in the algorithm previously described. The possible expansions for the node are then examined against the basic skeleton and the node variables, and expansions which are incompatible are eliminated. Then the constraints are considered. An expansion is compatible with a dominance constraint RES DOM A only if at least one of its nodes is an A or can dominate an A. If an expansion does not contain an A then the grammar is analyzed to determine for each node of the expansion whether it *must* dominate A, *can* dominate A, or *cannot* dominate A. Similarly, an expansion is compatible with a nondominance constraint RES NDOM B only if none of its nodes is a B and none must obligatorily dominate B. Expansions which contain the sentence symbol S are eliminated unless either an S is required by the basic skeleton, or there is a constraint RES DOM S.

Finally, an expansion is chosen at random from those that are left, and the tree and string are updated. In updating the tree, first the used node variables are removed and the additional nodes of the expansion are added. The dominance and nondominance constraints are then reconsidered. If a dominance constraint has been satisfied, or will now inevitably be satisfied, it is dropped; otherwise

Skeleton

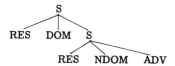

Current string: S

Expansion of main S.   The constraint is moved to a random choice among NP, VP, and ADV.

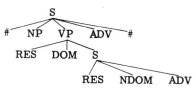

Current string: # NP VP ADV #

Expansion of VP.   The constraint is moved to MV, because AUX cannot dominate S.

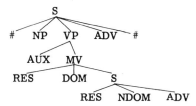

Current string: # NP AUX MV ADV #

Expansion of MV, AUX, and ADV's.   Choices are random, but do not introduce S. The constraint continues to move down.

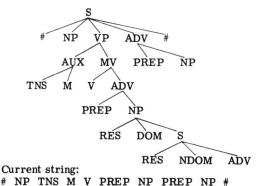

Current string:
NP TNS M V PREP NP PREP NP

Figure 13.   Steps in the generation of a tree

Expansion of rest of main S. **The constraint is dropped when satisfied.**

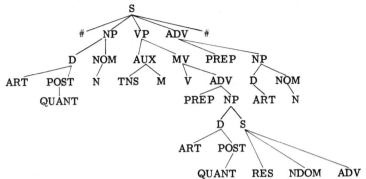

Current string:
ART QUANT N TNS M V PREP ART QUANT S PREP ART N

After main S is completed.

Current string: S

Expansion of embedded S. Constraint moved only to the VP, because PRE, NP cannot dominate ADV.

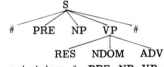

Current string: # PRE NP VP #

Expansion of VP. Constraint is no longer needed, since AUX, COP, AP cannot dominate ADV.

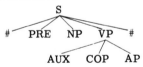

Current string: # PRE NP AUX COP AP #

Embedded subtree completed.

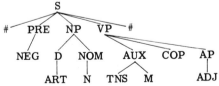

Current string: # NEG ART N TNS M COP ADJ #

Figure 13. Steps in the generation of a tree (cont.)

it is moved to a node selected at random from those that can later satisfy it. A nondominance constraint RES NDOM M is dropped when no further occurrence of M is possible; otherwise, copies of the constraint are attached to all the nodes of the current expansion that might dominate M. An important exception is that the dominance and nondominance constraints are never moved down over a sentence symbol.

The equality constraints are handled by expanding only the first node encountered with a particular equality constraint RES EQ i. Expansion of other nodes with RES EQ i is not carried out, but they are marked. Later, after the process of lexical insertion, copies of the first expansion are filled in for the other equal nodes.

CHAPTER 6

Complex Symbols

In this chapter we begin the presentation of a model of lexical insertion. It is based on the models proposed by Chomsky in *Aspects of the Theory of Syntax*, but does not attempt to replicate any one of them exactly. The development of the model brought out the close relation between lexical insertion and transformation, and led to a number of interesting problems; these would not have been seen without working out the details.

A complex symbol is a set of specifications of features or binary properties associated with a vocabulary word or with a node of a tree. The feature specifications determine the category of the word, the contexts in which it can occur, and various additional syntactic properties that affect its use.

*Complex-symbol*s occur in many formats of the syntax: *tree, structural-analysis, restriction, structural-change, lexical-entry* and *redundancy-rule*. *Structural-analyses* also occur in *contextual-features* and *contextual features* occur in *complex-symbol*s, so the discussion has an unavoidable circularity. In discussing the lexical component, we use the notion of analysis without giving a full description; a complete discussion is in Chapter 8. A minimum knowledge of the *lexicon* must also now be assumed, that is, that the lexicon contains *lexical-entry*s, which give *vocabulary-word*s and their *complex-symbol*s.

THE FORMAT

A complex symbol is usually shown graphically as a set of valued features or feature specifications enclosed in large square brackets. A typical complex symbol is:

$$\begin{bmatrix} +\text{N} \\ +\text{ANIMATE} \\ -\text{HUMAN} \\ +\text{SG} \\ \text{dog} \end{bmatrix}$$

In the computer model, a complex symbol is represented linearly; a sequence of feature specifications separated by blanks is enclosed between vertical bars.

4.01   *complex-symbol* ::= | list[*feature-specification*] |

4.02   *feature-specification* ::= *value feature*

4.07   *value* ::= + [] − [] *

53

Examples

> | +N +ANIMATE − HUMAN + SG |
>
> | +V +TRAN *PRET *FUTUR *PROG |

A complex symbol is an unordered set of feature specifications. A feature may occur only once in a complex symbol, because it is not meaningful to say of an occurrence of a word that it is, say, both +SINGULAR and −SINGULAR. The specification *SINGULAR means that the word is "either +SINGULAR or −SINGULAR," which is not the same thing.

The vocabulary word, e.g., "dog," does not occur in the *complex-symbol,* which contains only *feature-specifications.* The vocabulary word is given elsewhere, either as part of a lexical-entry, or a node name in a tree.

A *feature-specification* consists of a *feature* preceded by a *value.* For example, −ANIMATE is a *feature-specification* with the *value* − and the *feature* ANIMATE. *Feature-specifications* occur only within *complex-symbols.*

Three values are allowed for features. The third value * is an indefinite value; it indicates that the complex symbol is marked for the feature, but that the value is as yet unspecified. The * is roughly equivalent to ± but occasionally also functions as a variable. Its exact meaning is defined by its occurrences in the tables on p. 56 for complex symbol operations. The value * is never used with a contextual feature, because it would have no meaning there. The * never appears in a complex symbol in a tree; when a complex symbol is inserted in a tree, each * is changed to either + or −.

4.03 *feature* ::= *category-feature* [] *inherent-feature* []
      contextual-feature

4.04 *category-feature* ::= *word*

4.05 *inherent-feature* ::= *word*

4.06 *contextual-feature* ::= *word*

The three types of features are category features, inherent features, and contextual features. A feature may be denoted by any *word.* However, no *word* may be used for more than one feature.

A category feature is the name of a lexical category, such as noun (N) or verb (V). A complex symbol may not contain more than one positive feature specification for a category feature. Complex symbols in the entries of the lexicon must contain precisely one positively specified category feature, which indicates the type of lexical category node to which the complex symbol may be attached. A positive specification for one category feature implicitly specifies all other category features negatively.

If a word is of more than one category it may be given more than one complex symbol, each with one positive category feature. For example,

YARUK | +ADJ | "CLEAN"

YARUK | +V | "BECOME CLEAN"

Inherent features denote unanalyzable qualities such as HUMAN and ABSTRACT. An inherent feature can have the same name as a transformation, and so can be used to simulate a rule feature (Lakoff, 1965); Chapter 9 provides further discussion and an example.

A contextual feature, in contrast to an inherent feature, is not simply a name, but is analyzable. A *word* is a *contextual-feature* only if a *contextual-definition* identifies it with a *contextual-feature-description* that describes an environment for lexical insertion.

  7.07   *contextual-definition* ::=
          contextual-feature = *contextual-feature-description*

We discuss contextual features fully later in this chapter.

COMPLEX SYMBOLS IN TREES

The lexical insertion process puts complex symbols into trees; transformations may move or alter them. In lexical insertion, complex symbols are attached only to lexical category nodes. When a vocabulary word is selected for insertion, an associated complex symbol is merged with any that may already be on the lexical category node. The vocabulary word itself is attached as the daughter of the node. The example shows the position of complex symbols in a tree.

Example

In the lexicon the entry for BALL is

    BALL | +N −HUMAN −ANIMATE |

In the tree this complex symbol is no longer directly associated with BALL, but is attached to the N that dominates BALL.

Alternatives to attaching the complex symbols as shown here are to attach the complex symbol directly to the vocabulary word or to include the vocabulary word as part of the complex symbol. The advantages of our treatment are that it becomes possible to allow complex symbols at any node of the tree, and that— since they are node names—vocabulary words are available for mention in transformations. An example in which complex symbols appear at several levels in a tree is given in Chapter 8, in the discussion of the structural change known as "Chomsky-adjunction."

OPERATIONS

The basic operations for complex symbols are comparisons and changes.

Comparisons. Comparisons of complex symbols are needed in deciding whether a lexical entry can be inserted at a node, in testing the structural description of a transformation against a tree, and in testing restrictions. The model includes four basic comparisons: equality, non-distinctness, and two types of inclusion.

In comparing two complex symbols, the feature specifications for each feature are compared. The result of a test for a particular feature depends on the combination of the values +, — and * and also abs (absent). The comparison of the complex symbols succeeds only if it succeeds for every feature. The comparisons for complex symbols are:

> Two complex symbols are *equal* if they contain exactly the same feature specifications.

> Two complex symbols are *nondistinct* if all their feature specifications are nondistinct; that is, no feature has the value + in one and the value — in the other.[1]

> Complex symbol *n* is *included-1* in complex symbol *m* if each feature with positive or negative value in *n* occurs in *m* with like value, and if each feature that occurs in *n* with value * occurs in *m* with some value.

> Complex symbol *n* is *included-2* in complex symbol *m* if each feature specification in *n* also occurs in *m*.

These definitions are conveniently summarized by matrices; the entry indicates whether the result of the comparison is true (T) or false (F). The matrices for the four basic comparisons are:

n EQUALS *m*

n \ m	+	—	*	abs
+	T	F	F	F
—	F	T	F	F
*	F	F	T	F
abs	F	F	F	T

n NONDISTINCT FROM *m*

n \ m	+	—	*	abs
+	T	F	T	T
—	F	T	T	T
*	T	T	T	T
abs	T	T	T	T

---

[1] Category features are a special case. Two complex symbols are distinct if they are positively specified for different category features. We could have avoided this convention by using redundancy rules to indicate that if a complex symbol is positively specified for one category, it is negatively specified for all others, e.g., | +N | => | —V —COP —DET |. This rule exists implicitly although the expansion is never carried out.

n INCLUDED-1 IN m

n \ m	+	−	*	abs
+	T	F	F	F
−	F	T	F	F
*	T	T	T	F
abs	T	T	T	T

n INCLUDED-2 IN m

n \ m	+	−	*	abs
+	T	F	F	F
−	F	T	F	F
*	F	F	T	F
abs	T	T	T	T

In lexical insertion, the comparison is *compatibility*, which is defined later using the basic comparison of nondistinctness. In applying redundancy rules, the comparison is inclusion-1. The fact that neither + nor − is included-1 in * is important in that application. The model does not use equality or inclusion-2, which are provided for use in grammars.

Changes. The basic changes of complex symbols include merging n into m, erasing n from m, and saving only n in m. They are carried out one feature at a time, as are the comparisons. The changes are most easily expressed by their matrices; the entry is the final value for the feature in m after the change is made.

n MERGEF m

n \ m	+	−	*	abs
+	+	+	+	+
−	−	−	−	−
*	+	−	*	*
abs	+	−	*	abs

n ERASEF m

n \ m	+	−	*	abs
+	abs	−	−	abs
−	+	abs	+	abs
*	abs	abs	abs	abs
abs	+	−	*	abs

n SAVEF m

n \ m	+	−	*	abs
+	+	abs	+	abs
−	abs	−	−	abs
*	+	−	*	abs
abs	abs	abs	abs	abs

The change n ERASEF m causes the feature specifications of the complex symbol designated by n to be deleted from the complex symbol designated by m. The change n MERGEF m merges the feature specifications of n into the complex symbol m. If m is already specified for a feature which also occurs in n, the value in n overrides the old value. The change n SAVEF m deletes all feature specifications of m except for those which are common to n, which are saved. For example, after the change | *SG *PRO | SAVEF 6 the complex symbol designated by 6 contains the specifications for SG and PRO only, with their values unchanged.

The composite change n MOVEF m k moves the feature specifications common to the complex symbols n and m into complex symbol k. It is equivalent to n SAVEF m, m MERGEF k, except that m is not affected. The main use of this change is in agreement transformations. If the values in n are all indefinite, the effect is to make m and k agree for the features in n. For example | *SG | MOVEF 3 4 changes the value of the feature SG of the complex symbol denoted by 4 so that it is the same as that in 3. If 4 was not previously marked for SG a feature specification as in 3 is added. In any case, 3 is unchanged.

REDUNDANCY RULES

A redundancy rule adds feature specifications to complex symbols. Complex symbols are written in an abbreviated form, e.g., in the lexicon, and redundant feature specifications are added when the full form is needed. The redundancy rules of this model differ from those in *Aspects;* these are not generative, but abbreviatory. They are applied at any time in the entire process of sentence generation when a complex symbol is modified.

7.09   *redundancy-rule* ::= *complex-symbol* => *complex-symbol*

Examples of *redundancy-rules* are:

−MULT	=>	−PL
+PL	=>	+MULT
*PERS	=>	+HUMAN
*HUMAN	=>	+ANIM
+MULT −PL	=>	−ANIM
+MULT +ANIM	=>	+PL
*ABSTR	=>	−ANIM −MULT

The value * must not appear in the complex symbol on the right-hand side of a redundancy rule.

The interpretation of a redundancy rule is that any complex symbol that includes (using the test inclusion-1) the complex symbol on the left-hand side of the redundancy rule implicitly includes the complex symbol on the right. In the lexicon, these expansions remain implicit. However, for complex symbols in the tree, the expansions are made explicit. In fact, whenever a complex symbol in the tree is changed, the redundancy rules are again checked for possible further expansion.

The redundancy rules of a grammar are not ordered. When they are applied to expand a complex symbol the process terminates only when no further application is possible. For example, suppose the rules are as given, and the complex symbol

   | +N −ABSTR |

is to be expanded. The first rule which applies is the last one, which introduces

—ANIM and —MULT. Then the first rule can apply, and it introduces —PL. No more rules are relevant, so the result is

| +N —ABSTR —ANIM —MULT —PL |

In the case of a conflict between an explicit feature specification and an implicit specification by a redundancy rule, no change is made.

Notice that complex symbols, not just feature specifications, appear on both sides of redundancy rules. This makes it possible to have rules of the form | +A —B | => | +C |. This form, more general than the usual forms, seems more natural; it has advantages, but also makes the model more complicated than it would be otherwise. Having more than one feature specification on the left is particularly useful if one of the specifications is for a category feature. Then the entire process of checking redundancy rules is more efficient, since it is immediately apparent that the rule cannot apply to other categories. In addition, it is useful to be able to limit the implicit expansion to the case of a specific category. Given the rule | +HUMAN | => | +ANIMATE |, if the feature specification +HUMAN is moved from a noun to another category, say WH, the WH would implicitly be marked also as +ANIMATE. If it desired to avoid this and mark the WH only with +HUMAN the redundancy rule can be written | +N +HUMAN | => | +ANIMATE |.

Chomsky (1965) uses rules very similar in form to these redundancy rules in his first alternative for introducing complex symbols into trees. His rules, such as | +ANIMATE | → | ±HUMAN |, are not redundancy rules in the sense used here; rather, they are generative rules. The interpretation of the rule just given would be that any complex symbol containing the feature specification +ANIMATE must also be specified for the feature HUMAN. Rules of this form, which could be written | +ANIMATE | => | *HUMAN |, are not allowed in our interpretation, since this would mean that for any particular +ANIMATE vocabulary word the choice between +HUMAN and —HUMAN was arbitrary. For vocabulary words, this is not the case. Therefore, we do not allow redundancy rules in which the value * is used in the complex symbol on the right. [2]

A redundancy rule with the indefinite value * on the left is admissible. The rule

| *HUMAN | => | +ANIMATE |

is equivalent to the two rules

| +HUMAN | => | +ANIMATE |
| —HUMAN | => | +ANIMATE |

and may be regarded as an abbreviation for that pair of rules.

---

[2] In cases such as | +N | => | *SG | and | +V | => | *PROGRESSIVE |, a random choice of feature value does make sense. As the model now stands, this must be indicated in other ways. For example, *SG can be included in the complex symbol of the lexical entry, as in

NGOMBE NGURUWE CHUI NDEGE | +C7 +N *SG —HUMAN |
   "COW(S), PIG(S), TIGER(S), BIRD(S)"

We now observe why the result of the inclusion comparison for | —A | included in | *A | or | +A | included in |*A | must be false. For otherwise, the redundancy rule | —A | => |—B | would cause the complex symbol | *A | to be expanded to | *A —B | which is equivalent to | +A —B | or | —A —B |. Actually, the result of the application of the redundancy rule should be equivalent to | +A | or | —A —B |.

THE COMPATIBILITY TEST

Allowing redundancy rules to have complex symbols on the left-hand side complicates the testing of pairs of complex symbols. The basic test for lexical insertion cannot be nondistinctness but must be compatibility, defined as follows:

> Two complex symbols are *compatible* if (a) they are nondistinct, and (b) the application of the redundancy rules to the result of merging them does not lead to a conflict in the value of any feature.

To see that this criterion must replace nondistinctness as a test, notice the complex symbols | +A | and | —B —C | are nondistinct, but in the presence of the redundancy rule | +A —B | => | +C | they are not compatible.

The actual execution of the compatibility test is complicated by the possible presence of the value * in the complex symbol obtained when the pair of complex symbols is merged prior to expansion by the redundancy rules. The appearance of the value * denotes an abbreviation for two complex symbols, one positively specified for the feature and one negatively specified. In general, if the value * appears n times, the complex symbol is an abbreviation for 2^n complex symbols. To illustrate, in testing the complex symbols | +A +D | and | +A *B *C | for compatibility, it is established first that they are nondistinct. They are then merged, with the result | +A *B *C +D | which is an abbreviation for the four complex symbols

| +A +B +C +D |

| +A +B —C +D |

| +A —B +C +D |

| +A —B —C +D |

Now the redundancy rules may be such that all, some, or none of these possibilities are good. For example, if the redundancy rule | +B | => | —C | exists, then the first complex symbol is not a possible choice, but the remaining three are acceptable. Because there may be more than one compatible complex symbol, the compatibility test not only indicates compatibility or incompatibility, but also gives a resultant expanded complex symbol. When * values are present, the complex symbols are tested at random until a compatible result is found. This complex symbol is returned as part of the test. If all complex symbols fail when expanded by the redundancy rules, the test returns the value false to indicate incompatibility. Notice that the complex symbol that is the result of the compatibility test does not contain the value * . Thus, the value * never appears in a complex symbol inserted in the tree.

CONTEXTUAL FEATURES

Contextual features describe tree environments where a vocabulary word may appear. These descriptions are of essentially the same form as the structural descriptions for transformations. The contextual features in the model differ sharply from those in *Aspects,* both in form and in the conventions regarding their use. Contextual features include both subcategorization and selectional features as defined by Chomsky; we have not found it necessary to make the distinction explicit. A selectional feature would correspond to a contextual feature which contains at least one complex symbol.

A vocabulary word is specified for a contextual feature only if the feature must be checked to determine if the word can be inserted. A word without contextual features can thus appear at any appropriate category node. If a vocabulary word is positively specified for a contextual feature, the word can appear only in that context; if negatively specified, the word must not appear in that context.

This marking convention is not the one given in *Aspects.* Chomsky's convention is that the complex symbol includes a positive specification of a strict sub-categorization feature for every environment in which it is permissible to insert the word; the specification is negative (or absent) if the word must not be inserted. The subcategorization features are mutually exclusive; if the environment meets one, it will fail the others. His selectional features are negative if the word must not be inserted; they are positive (or absent) if the word may be inserted.

A *contextual-feature* is simply a name for the complete *contextual-feature-description.* The feature and the description are associated by a *contextual-definition* in the preliminary part of the lexicon.

Contextual feature descriptions are very similar to the structural descriptions of transformations, which makes it possible to use the same algorithms in evaluating both. A full discussion of the form of structural descriptions and the analysis algorithm appears in Chapter 8. Only points directly relevant to contextual features are discussed here.

2.02   *contextual-feature-description* ::=
⟨ *structure* opt[, WHERE *restriction*] ⟩

The *contextual-feature-description* contains a special case of *structural-description,* the *structure.* A *structure* defines an analysis of a specified *node,* called the "element" of the *structure.* It is required that the *element* of the *structure* in a *contextual-feature-description* be a specific node name, not a _ or * . Further, the *structure* must contain precisely one underline symbol _ which indicates the location of the category symbol for which a vocabulary word is to be inserted. This is perhaps best clarified by examples.

In the first examples to follow, the trees can be considered to have been generated according to the following phrase structure rules.

S   = # NP VP # .

VP = V (NP) .

NP = (DET) N.

The contextual feature TRANS could be defined by

$$\text{TRANS} = \langle \text{VP} \langle \_ \text{NP} \rangle \rangle$$

where the structure is VP $\langle$ _ NP $\rangle$ and its element is VP. The feature TRANS appearing in a complex symbol for a verb would indicate a transitive verb (+TRANS) or an intransitive verb (−TRANS). An examination of the following tree shows that the structure of the contextual feature TRANS is present. Thus a verb with the feature specification +TRANS would be suitable for insertion at the node V, and one with the feature specification −TRANS would not. A verb with no specification for the feature TRANS will be suitable for insertion in either this tree or one without an object.

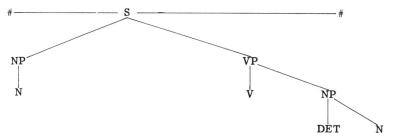

The contextual feature TRANS is an example of a strict local subcategorization feature, because the element VP immediately dominates the underline corresponding to V. A user who adheres to Chomsky's "principle of strict local subcategorization" will always use as the element of a contextual feature the node which immediately dominates the one at which the lexical insertion is to be made. A user who disavows this principle may choose any dominating node for the element.

The verb feature ANIMOBJ (animate object) would be defined by

$$\text{ANIMOBJ} = \langle \text{VP} \langle \_ \text{NP} \langle \% \text{N} \mid +\text{ANIMATE} \mid \rangle \rangle \rangle \; .$$

The *structure* contained in this feature is

$$\text{VP} \langle \_ \text{NP} \langle \% \text{N} \mid +\text{ANIMATE} \mid \rangle \rangle$$

It has the element VP. The "skip" symbol % is used to avoid specification of irrelevant material. The brackets are used as in the definition previously given for trees. So ANIMOBJ matches subtrees of the form

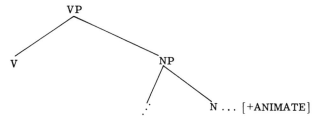

which are precisely those verb phrases with +ANIMATE objects.

The *contextual-feature* ANIMSUB could be defined by:

ANIMSUB = ⟨ S ⟨ # NP ⟨ % N | +ANIMATE | ⟩ VP ⟨ _ % ⟩ # ⟩ ⟩

A verb positively specified for this contextual feature can appear only in trees of the form:

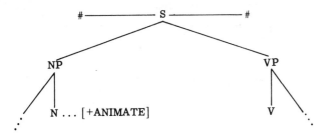

Notice that the element of the structure for ANIMSUB is S, and not the VP which immediately dominates V.

The next example illustrates the variety of forms of contextual feature descriptions. The relevant phrase structure rules are:

S   = # (PRE) NP AUX VP # .

VP = (HAVE EN) (BE ING) (V ((NP, PP)) ((S, PP)) (MAN) ,
     BE (ADJ)) .

NP = (DET) N (S) .

A set of contextual features for verbs (V) for this phrase structure might be:

```
V1 = <VP< % _ NP S ? >> ,
V2 = <VP< % _ NP (MAN)>>,
V3 = <VP< % _ PP ? >> ,
V4 = <VP< % _ S % >> ,
V5 = <VP< % _ (MAN)>> ,
V6 = <VP< % _ NP< N S >>>,
V7 = <S < # (PRE) NP< N S> AUX VP<% _ NP<% N|+ANIMATE|%>%>%>>,
V8 = <VP< % _ NP<(DET) N|+HUMAN|> PP<PREP NP<N S>> > > ,
V9 = <VP<%_NP PP (MAN)>>,
```

Several noteworthy points appear in this example. V2 specifies a context in which the node MAN is optional. Nonetheless, V2 is regarded as one feature, not as an abbreviation for two features as in *Aspects*. In V7, as in ANIMSUB, the element does not immediately dominate the category node for lexical insertion. The list lacks a feature of the form V10 = ⟨ VP ⟨ % _ % ⟩ ⟩ , for good reason. With the conventions of this model, +V10 would always be met and thus mean nothing; a verb marked −V10 would never be inserted in any possible tree.

Restrictions in contextual features

We extend the usual notion of contextual feature by allowing the description to optionally contain a restriction. The capability is included by analogy with the definition of structural descriptions for transformations. Integers may be assigned to terms within the *structure* and referred to in the restriction to impose further requirements on the environment. Contextual features with restrictions can be used to express "deep structure constraints" as discussed by Perlmutter (1968). For example, the verb "condescend" requires on his analysis that the subject noun phrase of the matrix sentence and that of the embedded sentence be the same. For a simplified phrase structure with the rules S = NP VP., VP = V (NP)., and NP = (S, N)., this constraint might be expressed by the feature LIKESUBJ:

$$\text{LIKESUBJ} = \langle\, \text{S} \,\langle\, 1\ \text{NP VP} \,\langle\, \_\ \text{NP} \,\langle\, \text{S} \,\langle\, 2\ \text{NP \%} \,\rangle\,\rangle\,\rangle\,\rangle\,, \text{WHERE } 1\ \text{EQ } 2\,\rangle$$

Notice that there is no difficulty in expressing a constraint that relates matrix and embedded sentences, because the *structure* that can appear in a *contextual-feature-description* is arbitrary and is not restricted to a description of the matrix sentence.

Contextual features as inherent features

Contextual features appearing in complex symbols that are embedded in contextual features are treated as though they were inherent features. Similarly, once a word has been inserted in the tree, its contextual features function as inherent only.[3]

When lexical insertion is complete, the major function of the contextual feature has been served. In many grammars, contextual features play no further part in sentence generation and could be removed from the complex symbol before it becomes part of the tree. However, contextual features describe the tree at the time of lexical insertion, before transformation. Therefore, we carry them into the tree, where they can be used as "memory" devices. A transformation may refer to the contextual features to determine the state of the tree at the time of lexical insertion even after other transformations have altered the tree.

---

[3] Contextual features are used in this double way in the following example. Suppose the phrase structure contains the rule

$$\text{AUX} = (\,\text{ASP}\,)\,(\,\text{M}\,)\,(\,\text{DUB}\,(\,\text{M}\,)\,,\text{M}\,)\,(\,\text{PAST}\,)\,(\,\text{QUES}\,)\,.$$

and the contextual features include ASP1, ASP2 for ASP, and M12, M13 for M:

$$\text{ASP1} = \langle\, \text{AUX} \,\langle\, \_\ (\,\text{M}\,)\ \text{DUB}\ (\,\text{M}\,)\ (\,\text{QUES}\,) \,\rangle\,\rangle$$
$$\text{ASP2} = \langle\, \text{AUX} \,\langle\, \_\ (\,\text{M}\,)\ (\,\text{DUB}\,)\ (\,\text{M}\,)\ (\,\text{QUES}\,) \,\rangle\,\rangle$$
$$\text{M12} = \langle\, \text{AUX} \,\langle\, \text{ASP} \mid +\text{ASP2} \mid \text{\%} \_ \,\rangle\,\rangle$$
$$\text{M13} = \langle\, \text{AUX} \,\langle\, \text{ASP} \mid +\text{ASP1} \mid \text{\%} \_ \,\rangle\,\rangle$$

Then the choice for ASP will affect the choice for M.

## CHAPTER 7

The Lexical Component

The lexical component consists of a lexicon and an algorithm that uses the lexicon in inserting vocabulary words into trees. The lexicon contains a preliminary part, or prelexicon, which includes the definitions of contextual features, lists of category and inherent features, and redundancy rules. Following the prelexicon come the lexical entries themselves. The lexical insertion algorithm selects lexical items from the lexicon and inserts them into the tree. The main points of interest are the order of lexical insertion, the use of the analysis process for contextual features, and the treatment of the side effects of a lexical insertion. This chapter describes the lexicon and discusses in detail the lexical insertion process.

THE LEXICON

The lexicon has two parts, the prelexicon and the lexical entries. The prelexicon contains feature definitions and redundancy rules. The lexical entries consist of the vocabulary words and their complex symbols.

> 7.01   *lexicon* ::= **LEXICON** *prelexicon lexical-entries* $

Full descriptions of the parts of a lexicon follow a simple example.

The lexicon in Figure 14 is constructed from examples given by Chomsky (1965). The phrase structure rules are included because the form of the contextual features depends on the phrase structure. The category order for lexical insertion is verbs (V), then nouns (N), and finally determiners (DET). Four features are defined as inherent: ABSTRACT, ANIMATE, COUNT, and HUMAN. The contextual features are TRANS (to distinguish transitive and intransitive verbs), COMMON (for nouns), ANIMSUB (for verbs taking +ANIMATE subjects), NANIMSUB (For verbs taking −ANIMATE objects), ANIMOBJ (for verbs taking +ANIMATE objects), NANIMOBJ (for verbs taking −ANIMATE objects), and NABSTOBJ (for verbs taking −ABSTRACT objects). Four redundancy rules are given, followed by a short list of lexical entries.

Prelexicon

The prelexicon contains feature definitions and redundancy rules:

> 7.02   *prelexicon* ::= *feature-definitions* opt[*redundancy-rules*]

> 7.03   *feature-definitions* ::=
>   *category-definitions* opt[*inherent-definitions*]
>   opt[*contextual-definitions*]

```
                    "  FRAGMENT FROM ASPECTS  "
PHRASESTRUCTURE
        S = # NP VP # .
        VP = V (NP) .
        NP = (DET) N .
$ENDPSG
LEXICON
        CATEGORY  V  N  DET  .
        INHERENT  ABSTRACT  ANIMATE  COUNT  HUMAN  .
        CONTEXTUAL
               TRANS = <VP<_NP>>,
               COMMON = <NP<DET_>>,
               ANIMSUB =  <S<#NP<%N|+ANIMATE|>VP<_%>#>>,
               NANIMSUB = <S<#NP<%N|-ANIMATE|>VP<_%>#>>,
               ANIMOBJ =  <VP<_NP<%N|+ANIMATE|>>>,
               NANIMOBJ = <VP<_NP<%N|-ANIMATE|>>>,
               NABSTOBJ = <VP<_NP<%N|-ABSTRACT|>>> .
        RULES
               |+COUNT| => |+COMMON|,
               |+ABSTRACT| => |+COMMON -ANIMATE|,
               |+HUMAN| => |+ANIMATE|,
               |+ANIMATE| => |-ABSTRACT| .
        ENTRIES
               SINCERITY VIRTUE  |+N -COUNT +ABSTRACT|,
               BOY  |+N +COUNT +HUMAN|,
               GEORGE BILL  |+N -COMMON -COUNT +HUMAN|,
               THE  |+DET| ,
               EAT  |+V +TRANS +ANIMSUB +NABSTOBJ|
                    |+V -TRANS +ANIMSUB|,
               GROW |+V +TRANS +ANIMSUB +ANIMOBJ|
                    |+V -TRANS +ANIMSUB|,
               FRIGHTEN |+V +TRANS +ANIMOBJ|,
               ELAPSE OCCUR |+V -TRANS +NANIMSUB|,
               ADMIRE |+V +TRANS +ANIMSUB|,
               READ |+V +TRANS +ANIMSUB +NANIMOBJ +NABSTOBJ| ,
               BUTTER |+N -COUNT -ABSTRACT -ANIMATE|,
               BOOK |+N -ANIMATE +COUNT| ,
               BEE |+N +COUNT +ANIMATE -HUMAN| ,
               WEAR |+V +NANIMOBJ|
                    |+V -TRANS +ANIMSUB| ,
               OWN |+V +TRANS +ANIMSUB +NABSTOBJ|,
               KNOW |+V +TRANS +ANIMSUB| ,
               EGYPT |+N -COMMON -COUNT -ANIMATE|,
               DOG |+N +COUNT -HUMAN +ANIMATE| ,
               CARROT |+N +COUNT +ANIMATE -HUMAN| ,
               RUN |+V +ANIMSUB| .
$ENDLEX
```

Figure 14. Example of lexicon

7. 04   *category-definitions* ::= CATEGORY list[*category-feature*].

7. 05   *inherent-definitions* ::= INHERENT list[*inherent-feature*].

An ordered list of category features is part of the feature definitions. This list must contain all categories for which lexical insertion is to be performed. The order in the list specifies the category order for insertion in the tree. For example, the *category-definitions*

CATEGORY V N COP DET.

specifies that verbs (V) are to be inserted first, followed by nouns (N), then copulas (COP), and then determiners (DET). The considerations involved in the choice of an order for the lexical categories are different in this model than in *Aspects*. A treatment of side effects of lexical insertion makes it unnecessary to insert a category with inherent features (say, N with feature ANIMATE) before a category that in turn refers to those features in its contextual features (say, V with contextual features ANIMSUB and ANIMOBJ containing the term N | +ANIMATE |). This point is clarified in the discussion of the lexical insertion process.

A list of inherent features may optionally be given as part of the *feature-definitions*. An example of *inherent-definitions* is

INHERENT MULT PL ANIM HUMAN PRO PERS
          FSTPERS ABSOL ABSTR SGSUF.

This list is optional because any feature not specifically defined as a particular type of feature is assumed to be inherent. However, the list is a convenient record of the inherent features in the grammar.

7. 06   *contextual-definitions* ::=
         CONTEXTUAL clist[*contextual-definition*] .

7. 07   *contextual-definition* ::=
         contextual-feature = *contextual-feature-description*

A contextual feature denoting, for example, commonness for nouns can be defined by

COMMON = < NP < DET _ > >

This *contextual-feature* can appear in a *complex-symbol*, as in

ELEPHANT | +N +COMMON |

rather than

ELEPHANT | +N + < NP < DET _ > > |

Although the syntax allows only *contextual-features* here, the output of the computer program shows the full *contextual-feature-descriptions*.

The use of a *contextual-definition* to relate a *contextual-feature* and a *contextual-feature-description* avoids the necessity of writing the complete *contextual-feature-description* each time the feature is used. Also, because contextual features are defined only once, updating the lexicon to reflect modifications in the phrase structure is not difficult. Only the *contextual-definitions* need be altered; the lexical entries are unchanged.

The redundancy rules for complex symbols are described in Chapter 6. The prelexicon contains their definitions:

> 7.08   *redundancy-rules* ::= RULES clist[*redundancy-rule*].

> 7.09   *redundancy-rule* ::= *complex-symbol* => *complex-symbol*

Lexical entries

Lexical entries constitute the major portion of the lexicon. A lexical entry is a set of vocabulary words, and an associated set of complex symbols, each of which contains exactly one positively specified category feature.

> 7.10   *lexical-entries* ::= ENTRIES clist[*lexical-entry*].

> 7.11   *lexical-entry* ::= list[*vocabulary-word*] list[*complex-symbol*]

> 7.12   *vocabulary-word* ::= *word*

Each complex symbol in a lexical entry represents a different sense in which the vocabulary words of the entry may be used. Each vocabulary word may be paired with any one of the complex symbols. Thus, the complex symbol set is interpreted as a disjunction of complex symbols. Because a complex symbol is interpreted as a conjunction of feature specifications, we have, in effect, a normal form in which any logical combination of complex symbols and feature specifications may be represented. Thus the system has the same power as one which allows arbitrary Boolean combinations of features (see Lakoff, 1965). For example, to say that a verb must have both an animate subject and an inanimate object, one may use either one or two *feature-specifications* in the same *complex-symbol*. To say that it must have either an animate subject or an inanimate object, two *complex-symbols* are needed.

The pair consisting of a word and a complex symbol is referred to as a "lexical item." It is lexical items that are selected from lexical entries for insertion in the tree. Thus, the lexical entry

BIJITUKAN SENDAI TENGOKU TOKYO | +N +LOCATE |

represents four lexical items. This form for the lexical entry makes possible a compact representation, and can serve to indicate that certain vocabulary words have the same syntactic properties. However, if desired, each lexical item may be written as a distinct lexical entry.

To simplify the selection of items from the lexicon, all lexical entries of a particular category are linked together. This does not mean that the *lexical-entry*s must be grouped by category; the program constructs the hierarchial structure. However, it does mean that for grammars to be run with the computer program, the complex symbols in any one lexical entry must have the same category feature. For example, the lexicon may contain the two entries

A7AYE | +A +A1 | , A7AYE | +N +N3 | "GOOD"

but may not contain just the single entry

A7AYE | +A +A1 | | +N +N3 | "GOOD"

THE LEXICAL INSERTION ALGORITHM

Lexical insertion occurs after the generation of a preterminal string by the phrase structure component and before transformation.

Chomsky (1965) proposes two styles of lexical insertion. In the first, complex symbols, including inherent and contextual features, are introduced by rewriting rules. A lexical item is suitable for insertion if its complex symbol is nondistinct from a complex symbol in the tree. The alternative does not introduce complex symbols by rewriting rules. Rather, a lexical item is suitable if its complex symbol is nondistinct from a tree complex symbol *and* if each contextual feature specification in the complex symbol is met by the tree. Chomsky remarks (*Aspects*, p. 122) that the contextual features may be thought of as the Boolean structure index (structural description) of a transformation, and that the insertion of a lexical item can be viewed as a substitution transformation. It is not clear from his discussion whether he intends lexical insertion to be merely thought of as a transformation, or actually implemented as a transformation.

In our interpretation, lexical insertion is independent of the transformation phase, although there is much in common between the two. The separation was made for several reasons. First, studying the insertion process should lead to better understanding of its basic nature. Second, the analysis performed for a contextual feature differs slightly from the analysis performed for a transformation. These differences are considered further in Chapter 8. Third, a complex symbol may contain more than one contextual feature, each of which is a type of structural description. Thus, to specify a conjunction of contextual features as a structural description for a transformation, it is necessary either to combine all contextual features into a single inclusive feature, or to allow conjunctions of structural descriptions to appear in transformations. Also, there is no convenient way to specify the selection of a vocabulary word as part of the structural change of a transformation. If the vocabulary words are included in the transformation, the concept of a lexicon as a distinct entity is lost.

Order

If a tree has embedded sentence subtrees, they are considered in lowest to highest, left to right order. In the following example, subtrees would be considered in order as numbered.

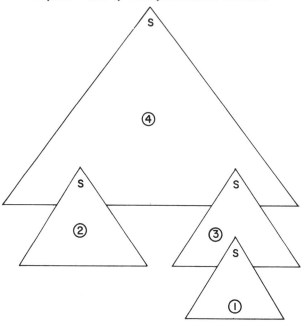

Within a sentence subtree, a lexical item is inserted at each lexical category node appearing in the subtree. The category nodes are considered by type in the order specified in the lexicon. In each category, the order is left to right in the tree. Thus, if the lexicon defined the category order as V N DET, the nodes in the following tree would be considered in the order shown by the numbers.

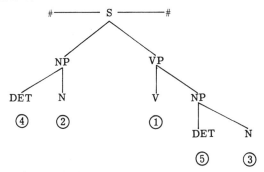

The order in which categories are considered can affect the efficiency of the insertion algorithm. That is, more or fewer lexical entries may have to be tested before a suitable complex symbol is located. Vocabulary words are selected at random; the same terminal strings will not be obtained for the same random numbers when different category orders are used. However, any string which can be obtained with one category order can also be obtained with any other category order. An example is given below.

Selection

For each lexical category node in the tree, the lexicon is searched to find a vocabulary word with a complex symbol that permits insertion. Since the lexical entries are linked by category, it is possible to search the lexicon considering only entries in the proper category. A lexical item is to be selected from the set of all items acceptable for insertion. It would be inefficient to form a complete list of those items and then choose from it. Therefore, a different method of selection has been devised.

This method tests random entries in the following manner. An entry is selected at random from the list of entries of the appropriate category. Each entry may contain many complex symbols; each one is compared with the complex symbol associated with the category node. When one is found which is compatible with the complex symbol in the tree, its contextual features are examined. An analysis of the tree is performed for each contextual feature specification to determine if the tree has the desired structure. In the analysis, the underline _ in the contextual feature must correspond to the category node. If the contextual feature contains embedded complex symbols, they are compared for compatibility with the corresponding complex symbols in the tree. Since the analysis of a contextual feature can be complicated, it is performed only once for any contextual feature. The value of the feature is saved in case the contextual feature appears in another complex symbol that is tested for insertion at the same node.

When all acceptable complex symbols in an entry are found, one is selected at random. A vocabulary word is then selected at random from the list of vocabulary words for the entry. This vocabulary word and the complex symbol that is the result of the compatibility test form the lexical item that will be inserted in the tree.

If the lexical entry does not contain an acceptable complex symbol, the number of entries to be tested is reduced by one and the entry examined is marked so that it will not be retested. Another entry is then selected at random from those that remain, and the process continues. The process terminates when an acceptable lexical item is selected, or when no more entries remain to be tested. In the latter case, there is no acceptable item for insertion at the node, and the insertion algorithm continues with the next node to be considered.

This method of selection weights lexical entries equally. Since an entry may include more than one complex symbol, complex symbols do not have exactly equal probabilities of being selected. If this is an important consideration, the lexicon should be defined so that each entry consists of a single complex symbol with its associated vocabulary words. If the lexical items are to have equal probability of selection, the lexicon should be defined so that each entry is a single vocabulary word and a single complex symbol.

Insertion

The vocabulary word selected is inserted as a daughter of the category node. The complex symbol obtained as a result of the compatibility test is attached to the category node. Suppose the lexical item selected is

WAHHI7 | +N *MULT +ANIM | "COYOTE"

and the redundancy rules

$$| -MULT | => | -PL |$$

and

$$| +MULT +ANIM | => | +PL |$$

are defined. The item is suitable for insertion in either of the following subtrees.

There are two possible results of the compatibility test:

$$| +N -MULT +ANIM -PL | and | +N +MULT +ANIM +PL |.$$

Suppose that the first complex symbol is selected in the compatibility test. Then after lexical insertion the result is the same for either of the above NP's:

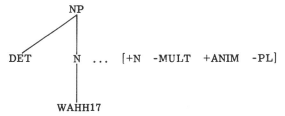

Side effects

The process of inserting a lexical item is now complete, except for the treatment of side effects. Side effects must be considered when a complex symbol containing a contextual feature with an internal complex symbol is inserted. An example is the feature ANIMSUB defined in the lexicon of Figure 14. This feature appears in the complex symbol for the verb ADMIRE. This verb is suitable for insertion in the base tree shown, because the subject noun is unspecified for the feature ANIMATE and thus compatible (nondistinct), as required.

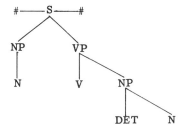

Once the verb has been inserted, the choice of subject is no longer arbitrary. To insure that an ANIMATE noun will be chosen, the appropriate node is now given the specification +ANIMATE. This is done by attaching to it the complex symbol obtained in the compatibility test during the original analysis for the contextual feature ANIMSUB.

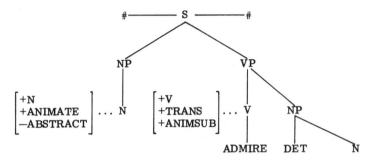

At a later stage in the lexical insertion process a noun is picked for the subject. A possible choice from the limited grammar of Figure 14 might be BILL. The complex symbol for the subject noun would then become

| +N +ANIMATE −ABSTRACT −COMMON −COUNT +HUMAN |

Notice that any result which could be obtained here by inserting the verbs (V) before the nouns (N) could also have been obtained in carrying out the lexical insertion in the order N V, and conversely. The choice of order does not change the class of possible trees, but it affects the efficiency of the process. It is also possible that for some orders the process can block, with no items acceptable for insertion at a given node. For the grammar of Figure 14, if the order is V N, then no matter what verb is selected, it is easy to find appropriate nouns to complete the tree, because there are both +ANIMATE and −ANIMATE nouns in the lexicon, and only that feature need be checked. However, if the nouns were chosen first it would be more difficult to find an appropriate verb, since contextual features would need to be checked. If, say, −ANIMATE nouns are selected for both noun nodes, then of the ten verb entries in the lexicon only one item WEAR | +V +NANIMOBJ | is acceptable.[1]

The treatment of side effects is not complete. The generality of the definition of the *structure* of a *contextual-feature-description* allows complex descriptions of environments. If negations (⌐) appear in the feature description, appropriate action is difficult to determine. Side effects may also be induced by the *restriction* in the feature description, but a thorough treatment is difficult.[2] The prin-

---

[1] If the lexicon were better, perhaps no item would be acceptable.

[2] In the current implementation of the algorithm, side effects are not treated if they are introduced by a restriction. The need for side effects can often be avoided by changing the order of lexical insertion so that the restriction can be definitely decided at the time it is first tested. For example, a feature qualified by 1 EQ 2 will work without side effects if all lexical insertion in 1 and 2 has been completed when the restriction is tested.

ciple issue is clear however; the insertion of a lexical item may produce effects on other nodes in the tree that must be accounted for if a grammatical sentence is to be obtained.

Negatively specified contextual features

A negatively specified contextual feature implies that the environment described by the feature must not be present. The interpretation is clear when the contextual feature does not contain complex symbols. But if one attempts to describe a verb that must take an inanimate subject by the feature specification —ANIMSUB, where ANIMSUB is the contextual feature defined in Figure 14, difficulties are encountered. First, the tree just given, prior to any lexical insertion, satisfies this feature. Thus, every lexical item with the feature specification —ANIMSUB would be rejected. This is clearly not what is desired. Note, however, that if a new contextual feature NANIMSUB is defined as in Figure 14, and if the complex symbol contains the feature specification +NANIMSUB, then the complex symbol would be acceptable, at least for this feature. Further, the subject noun would be correctly specified as —ANIMATE by side effects. The introduction of new contextual features which can be used positively to avoid negative contextual features is always possible.

One might propose that the lexical insertion algorithm perform a function similar to treating side effects when a negatively specified contextual feature with an embedded complex symbol is encountered. This might be an attempt to modify the tree so that the contextual feature would fail. This could easily be done in the previous example by specifying the subject noun as —ANIMATE. The tree would fail for the feature ANIMSUB and a complex symbol marked —ANIMSUB would be acceptable. Such a proposal encounters difficulties. For example, the tree shown below would also fail for the feature ANIMSUB, since an NP dominating an N is not present.

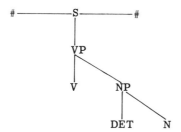

Therefore, a verb with the feature specification —ANIMSUB would be acceptable for insertion in this tree, as well. This may not be desirable and is not what was intended by the definition of the feature. We conclude that contextual features containing complex symbols should be positively specified.

If contextual features such as ANIMSUB are negatively specified, they are treated in the following manner. No attempt is made to cause the feature to fail. Thus if verbs are inserted before nouns, as in the example, no verb with the feature specification —ANIMSUB would ever be acceptable for insertion in a tree. Note, however, that if nouns are inserted before verbs, the feature specification —ANIMSUB will be treated as intended. Therefore, category order in which items are inserted could be important if negatively specified features are used. Side effects for negatively specified contextual features are not considered.

LEXICAL INSERTION WITH DIRECTED RANDOM SENTENCE GENERATION

The algorithm for directed random generation of base trees described in Chapter 5 can be used to produce inputs to the lexical insertion process. Some of the methods for constraining the form of the base tree may have an effect on lexical insertion and must be discussed briefly.

The form desired for the base tree is indicated by a "skeleton," which is actually a portion of the base tree with certain constraints. The complete base tree is built around the skeleton by random selection of appropriate phrase structure rules. The lexical insertion process may be affected in several ways. First, if the skeleton contains complex symbols, these complex symbols must be considered in lexical insertion. Second, there may be restrictions demanding equality of terminal nodes. Third, the skeleton may contain particular vocabulary words. To handle the last two cases, the lexical insertion process is modified slightly. A preliminary pass through the lexical insertion algorithm is executed treating only these effects. If vocabulary words are given in the tree, their corresponding complex symbols must be located and inserted in the tree and their side effects treated. Without this special consideration, the processing of side effects for other nodes might insert an incorrect feature specification into the complex symbol of a vocabulary word already present in the skeleton. If there are equality constraints in the skeleton, lexical items are selected and inserted to satisfy these constraints. After these special cases have been treated, the lexical insertion process is executed again to complete the tree.

CHAPTER 8

Analysis, Restriction, and Change

A transformation can apply to a tree only if the tree meets the structural description of the transformation. A vocabulary word can be inserted in a tree only if the tree satisfies the appropriate contextual feature descriptions. Since both the structural description and the contextual feature description ask the question, "Does the present tree have this given structure?" they can be treated in the same manner for most purposes. The similarity of the two becomes even more apparent when it is noted that both structural descriptions in transformations and contextual feature descriptions are composed of the same subparts, namely, structural analyses and restrictions. In this chapter the phrase "structural description" will be used ambiguously to refer to either. The tree is said to be *analyzab* e as the structural description if the answer to the question is affirmative. The process of answering the question is *analysis;* the resulting match of nodes in the tree with their counterparts in the structural description is *an analysis of* the tree as the structural description.

In the first part of this chapter we define the notion of structural description and give the conditions under which a tree may be said to be analyzable as a given structural description. Later we discuss in detail the algorithm which determines the order in which the various possible analyses of a tree are produced. The related concepts of structural change and restriction are also defined and discussed.

THE FORMAT

The notation for structural descriptions is described here; its meaning is given later. The formal definitions of structural description and contextual feature description are:

2.01   *structural-description* ::=
         structural-analysis opt[, WHERE *restriction*]

2.02   *contextual-feature-description* ::=
         ⟨ *structure* opt[, WHERE *restriction*] ⟩

For the first set of examples we use the *structural-description* (1) and the *contextual-feature-description* of ANIMSUB (2).

% AUX ⟨ % 3 T ⟩ 4 (BE, HAVE) % #   (1)

⟨ S ⟨ # NP ⟨ % N | +ANIMATE | ⟩ VP ⟨ _ % ⟩ # ⟩ ⟩   (2)

Although in this section we are concerned only with notation, it may help to know
that (1) is satisfied by, for example, the tree

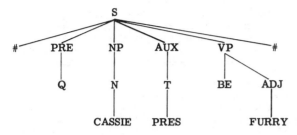

and that (2) matches either of the following, with the underline matching V.

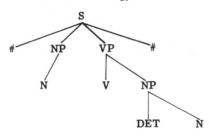

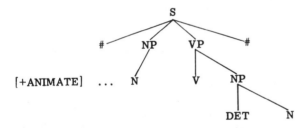

2.03   *structural-analysis* ::= list[*term*]

In a transformation, structural analysis plays essentially the same role as the
"structural description" and "structural analysis" first used by Chomsky.
However, it includes more powerful notations for describing tree structure than
have previously been given. The *structural-analysis* contained in (1) is all of
(1), because the optional part of a *structural-description* is omitted.

2.04   *term* ::=
         opt[*integer*] *structure* [] opt[*integer*] *choice* [] *skip*

2.05   *structure* ::=
         element opt[*complex-symbol*] opt[opt[¬]
         opt[/] ⟨ *structural-analysis* ⟩]

2.06   *element* ::= *node* [] * [] _

2.07   *choice* ::= (clist [*structural-analysis*])

2.08   *skip* ::= %

Term. The *structural-analysis* (1) contains six *terms*: # ; %; AUX ⟨ % 3 T ⟩ ; 4 (BE, HAVE) ; %; and # . The first and last *terms* (#) are *nodes*, hence *elements*, hence *structures*. *Terms* two and five (%) are *skips*. The term AUX ⟨ % 3 T ⟩ is a *structure* with the *element* AUX and the *structural-analysis* % 3 T. Finally the *term* 4 (BE, HAVE) is of the form *integer choice*.

Numbering of terms. Notice that the definition of *term* does not require that all *terms* contain *integers*; the numbering is used for reference in *restrictions* and *structural-changes*; if no reference is to be made to a *term*, it need not contain an *integer*. *Terms* which are *skips* must not be numbered. There are two additional constraints on the use of *integers* in *terms*. If the same *integer* is used for two *terms*, it must be the case that at most one of those *terms* can be nonnull in any analysis. Also no *term* may be governed by two *integers*, as in 2 (3V, 4ADJ). The use of integers in the model is a significant change from standard notation. It results from the treatment of transformations as changes of position of specific subtrees rather than rearrangements of the whole tree. This follows the approach taken in the MITRE grammars (Zwicky *et al.*, 1965).

Structure. The *structure* in (2) is

S ⟨ # NP ⟨ % N | +ANIMATE | ⟩ VP ⟨ _ % ⟩ # ⟩   (3)

The *element* here is S, and the *structural-analysis* of that S is

NP ⟨ % N | +ANIMATE | ⟩ VP ⟨ _ % ⟩ #   (4)

There are four *terms* in (4):

; NP ⟨ % N | +ANIMATE | ⟩ ; VP ⟨ _ % ⟩ ; and # . The second and third of these are *structures*, and could be further decomposed. Other examples of *structures* are:

SV / ⟨ _ COMPL ⟨ 1 SN S / ⟨ % 2SN V % ⟩ ⟩ ⟩

NP ¬⟨ NP ⟩

∗ ⟨ (PREP NP / ⟨ WH % ⟩ , NP / ⟨ WH % ⟩) ⟩

It may be noted that a *tree* is a special case of *structure* in which none of the special symbols ( ) ¬ % _ / or *integers* occur.

Element. The most common *element* is the *node*, which may be used wherever an *element* is needed. The *element* ∗ is an unspecified single node, i.e., a variable over single nodes. The *element* ∗ can always be distinguished by context from the *value* ∗. The *element* _ (underline) may appear only within a *contextual-feature-description*, where it indicates the node at which lexical insertion is to be performed. The *element* of the main *structure* of a *contextual-feature-description* may only be a *node*. It is essential that any *structure* begin with an *element*. For example, the sequences

(VP, AP) ⟨ % S % ⟩ and % ¬⟨ % # % ⟩

are not allowed even though there are natural interpretations for them.

Choice. *Choice* is illustrated by the (BE, HAVE) of (1), which is a (followed by a clist BE, HAVE followed by a). Each *structural-analysis* in this clist is a list of exactly one *term,* which is a *structure* without any preceding *integer.* Each of these *structures* is an *element* without any of the optional items, and each *element* is a *node.* Since a clist may be of length one, the *term* (PRE) is also a *choice.*

Skip. The *skip* replaces the variables of the conventional notation. The symbol % was chosen rather than X, Y, and Z because those letters are possible *nodes,* and because there is no need for more than one symbol. The use of a special symbol reinforces the idea that a variable need not correspond to a single subtree. As noted, a *skip* may not be preceded by an *integer.* As a consequence, *skips* may not be referred to in a *restriction,* nor in a *structural-change.* (The element * matches a single subtree and can be numbered.) The use of *skips* is subject to two constraints not stated in the formal description: Two adjacent *terms* of a *structural-analysis* must not both be *skips,* and each *structural-analysis* in the clist [*structural-analysis*] of a *choice* must contain at least one *term* which is not a *skip.*

The foregoing description does not explain the meaning of these formats, it simply describes how to write them. The meaning of structural descriptions and contextual feature descriptions is defined by their use in the analysis process, where each description serves as a template against which a tree can be matched.

Although a *structural-description* contains a *structural-analysis* and a *contextual-feature-description* contains a *structure,* the recursiveness of the definitions makes them very similar. The main difference stems from the fact that when transformations are being applied the position of the top node of the current tree is known, while during lexical insertion only the terminal node at which insertion is being attempted is known. For this reason, the contextual feature must specify the label of a node somewhere above the insertion node which can serve as the tree top. The *element* of the *structure* of the *contextual-feature-description* fills this role. Of course, in the contextual feature description there is also an underline _ which is the indicator of the position for the lexical insertion.

ANALYZABILITY

We define analyzability first for a *structural-analysis* or *structure* without an associated *restriction.* A later section considers how the presence of a *restriction* modifies the definition.

If a structural description is simply a list of *elements,* as in (5), analyzability is similar to Chomsky's notion of "proper analysis" (1957).

> # NEG Q NP AUX * #   (5)

A tree is analyzable as a structural description of this form if a one-to-one match of tree nodes with all of the structural description *elements* can be found such that:

1. Each terminal node in the tree is, or is dominated by, exactly one tree node in the match.

2. Left-to-right order of *elements* corresponds to left-to-right order of matching tree nodes.

3a. For each *element* which is a *node,* the label of the matching tree node is the same as the *node.*

3b. For each *element* which is a ＿ , the matching tree node is the node at which lexical insertion is currently being attempted.

3c. The *element* * matches any one tree node, regardless of its label.

A match of (5) with the tree nodes in (6) is indicated here by underlining the nodes in the match.

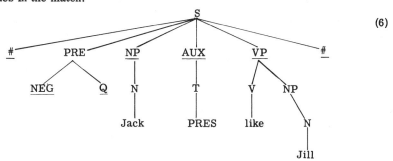

(6)

A *complex-symbol* following an *element* requires that there be a corresponding complex symbol attached to the matching tree node. "Corresponding" has a different meaning for lexical insertion than for transformations; in the case of lexical insertion the test is compatibility (roughly, no conflicting feature specifications; see Chapter 6 for a precise definition), while for transformations the test is inclusion (that is, the *complex-symbol* in the *structural-description* is included-1 in the one in the tree).

For example, the *contextual-feature-description*

⟨ VP ⟨ ＿ NP ⟨ DET N | +ANIMATE | ⟩ ⟩ ⟩

matches either of the subtrees (7) or (8)

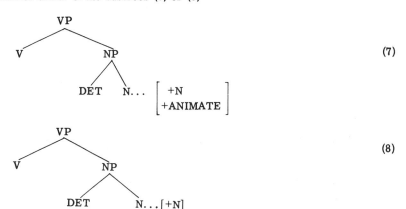

(7)

(8)

However, the very similar *structural-description*

% VP ⟨ V NP ⟨ DET | +ANIMATE | ⟩ ⟩ %

matches a tree containing the subtree (7) but does not match one containing
subtree (8).

A *skip* (the % symbol) is a variable which matches not just a single node, but any
string of adjacent terminal nodes. It may match a string of zero nodes, in which
case it is said to be null. The "range" of a *skip* is defined in terms of the
elements on either side; it is the set of tree nodes which dominate (or equal) the
nodes matching the *skip* and do not dominate the nodes matched by these side
*element*s. In other words, the range of a *skip* is precisely those tree nodes
which would have to be deleted if the *skip* were not present in order to leave the
analysis unchanged.

The matching of a *choice* is somewhat more complex. The procedure depends
on whether the clist within the choice has only one *structural-analysis*, or more
than one. If there is only one *structural-analysis*, the choice is an option; that
is, the tree is analyzable either if it is analyzable as a similar structural description without the parentheses of the choice, or if it is analyzable as a similar
structural description without any of the choice being present. Thus, NP (AUX)
VP matches either of the trees:

If there is more than one *structural-analysis* in the clist, a tree is analyzable
if it is analyzable as a similar structural description with some one of the
structural-analyses in place of the *choice*. (Note that the only requirement
here is that at least one *structural-analysis* will match; if several different
ones could be substituted it means that the tree is analyzable as this structural
description in several ways.) Thus, NP (VP, COP) matches either of the trees:

If a *structure* contains a *structural-analysis* within angle-brackets, as in the
term AUX ⟨ % 3 T ⟩ of (1), the bracketed *structural-analysis* is a "subanalysis"
of the *element*. This adds a requirement on analyzability of the subtree headed
by the tree node which matches the *element*. The subanalysis differs slightly
from an ordinary analysis of a tree. The top node of the subtree, which has
already been matched to the element, is not allowed to match any term within
the subanalysis. Otherwise, subanalysis is primarily a recursive application
of the definition of analysis. The exact requirement of the subanalysis depends
on the presence of the optional modifiers ⌐ (negation) and / (nonimmediacy).
If only the / is present, the analysis is made in the usual sense. If neither
modifier is present, the analysis is subject to the further requirement that any

element in the *structural-analysis* must match a tree node which is immediately dominated by the top node of the subtree. (The decision to use immediate dominance as the unmarked case here was made to preserve the notational similarity between *structure* and *tree*.) If a ⌐ modifier is present, then the subtree must *not* be analyzable in the sense just defined.

The *structure* AUX ⟨ % T ⟩ matches (9) but not (10):

(9)

(10)

The *structure* NP / ⟨ DET BOY ⟩ matches both (11) and (12):

(11)

(12)

The *sentence-symbol* S plays a special role in analyzability. Unless otherwise specified the analysis must be found without going into a subtree headed by the sentence symbol (an embedded sentence). The structural description

% A / ⟨ B % C % ⟩ % E %   (13)

matches the tree on the left but not the one on the right

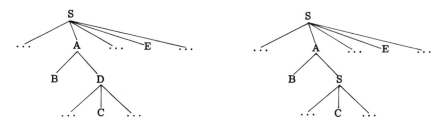

If it is desired to include an embedded sentence then the S of that sentence must be specifically mentioned in the structural description. If the structural description above is changed to

A / ⟨ B S ⟨ % C % ⟩ ⟩ % E %

then it will be matched only by the tree on the right.

This treatment of embedded sentences has the advantage that it specifies the exact depth of embedding at which a node is to be found, and further that it specifies exactly which part of the structural description may be matched to an embedded tree. One alternative is simply to mark the transformation as "embedding," in which case the structural description (13) would match either of the former trees, and would also match these:

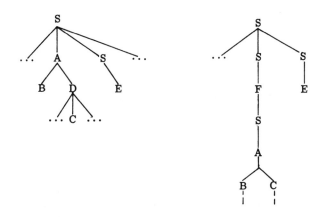

This alternative appears to be too broad; some intermediate compromise would probably be more satisfactory. These matters are receiving much attention in current linguistic work; recent work of Ross (1967) and Postal (1968) suggests that at least two distinct conventions are needed.

The negation modifier (¬) has been used only rarely in the grammars which have been constructed according to the computer model. However, one of its uses is important: ¬ seems to be necessary to define the concept of a "lowest sentence." Using a restriction which means that the tree node matching 1 must dominate a boundary symbol, a lowest sentence can be defined as one which matches the first S in the structural description

1 S ¬ / ⟨ % S ⟨ # % # ⟩ % ⟩ , WHERE 1 DOM # .

This definition presupposes a phrase structure in which the boundary symbols are introduced by a first rule of the form S = # ... # . The use of this definition of lowest sentence is discussed in Chapter 9.

The *contextual-feature-definition*

ANIMSUB = ⟨ S ⟨ # NP ⟨ % N | +ANIMATE |⟩ VP ⟨ _ % ⟩ # ⟩⟩

contains a *contextual-feature-description* which matches the tree:

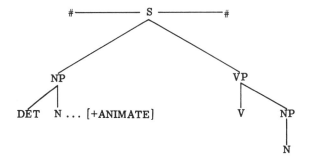

Integers do not directly enter into the analysis process; they permit reference to tree nodes in a restriction or a structural change. An *integer* preceding a *structure* is associated with the subtree headed by the tree node which matches the *element* of the *structure*. An *integer* preceding a *choice* is handled exactly as if it had been written at the beginning of every *structural-analysis* in the clist of the *choice*. Note that complex symbols are not numbered directly; the *integer* attaches to the tree node and refers to the complex symbol associated with that node in any context that requires a complex symbol.

ANALYSIS ALGORITHM

This section discusses the algorithm used to find a particular analysis of a tree as a structural description. The algorithm incorporates the definition of analyzability given on p. 79. The reason for giving the algorithm in detail is that it determines the order in which several possible analyses are taken if a tree can be analyzed in more than one way as a particular structural description. This is particularly important if the transformation specifies that only one analysis is to be found.

Analysis commences with a tree marker pointing to the top node of the tree and a structural description marker pointing to the first entity in the structural description. The procedure depends on the nature of this entity. *Integers* and *skips* are skipped but remembered. For an *element* (i.e., the beginning of a *structure*), a match to the node pointed to by the tree marker is attempted. A * matches any tree node, a *node* matches a node with the same label, and a _ matches the current lexical insertion node. If there is not a match, the tree marker is moved to point to the leftmost daughter of the current node, and matching is attempted again. This is repeated until either it is successful, or a terminal node is reached. If no match is found and no *skip* precedes the current *element*, the backtrack procedure (described below) is entered. If a *skip* precedes, the tree marker is moved to the top of the tree branch just right of the current branch, and matching is attempted again; in this case, the backtrack procedure is entered only if no match can be found for the rightmost terminal node of the tree.

If a match is found and a *complex-symbol* follows the *element*, it is compared to the complex symbol attached to the matching tree node for compatibility (in a contextual feature description) or inclusion (in a structural description). If the comparison fails, the analysis proceeds as though the tree node had not matched the *element*.

If an *integer* precedes the *element*, the *restriction* must be checked. In treating a *restriction* a three-valued logic is used. The value of the restriction is "undefined" until the analysis has proceeded far enough to determine a value of "true" or "false" for the whole restriction. Failure of the restriction again causes the analysis to proceed as though the node had not matched the element.

If the structural description marker is pointing to a *choice* instead of an *element*, the procedure to be followed depends on whether the clist of the *choice* contains only one *structural-analysis* (an option), or more than one (a true choice). For an option, the (of the choice is ignored; options affect only the backtrack procedure. For a true choice, a more complicated procedure is necessary. First, a list is made of all *elements* which could possibly be first in the choice, in left-to-right order. For example, if the choice were (A, (B) (C, D), % E, % (F, G)), this list would be A - B - C - D - E - F - G. The element-matching procedure is then followed as described above, but at each tree node all of the possible *elements* are tested for matches and for satisfactory *complex-symbols* and *integers*. Naturally, only those *elements* which are preceded by skips are tested after a terminal-node failure. When a satisfactory match is found between a tree node and some *element*, analysis proceeds along the associated *structural-analysis* of the *choice*, and after it is completed it continues with the part of the structural description that follows the *choice*.

If a *structural-analysis* within angle brackets follows an *element* that has been satisfactorily matched, a record is made of relevant information about the current status of the analysis, and analysis commences again, using the angle-bracketed *structural-analysis* and the subtree headed by the node matched to the *element*. If no / precedes, the tree marker is only allowed to point to immediate daughters of the top node during this analysis, instead of looking all the way down to terminal nodes. If a ⌐ precedes and the subtree is not analyzable, or if no ⌐ precedes and the subtree is analyzable, analysis continues following the angle-bracketed *structural-analysis;* otherwise, analysis proceeds as if the head *element* had not matched its tree node.

When a *structure* has been successfully matched, the tree marker is moved to point to the top node of the tree branch immediately to the right of the tree node matching the head *element*, and analysis proceeds. The tree is analyzable as the structural description if the rightmost *element* not within angle brackets successfully matches a tree node on the rightmost branch of the tree, or if the rightmost such *element* has been successfully matched in any way and a *skip* follows it.

The backtrack procedure is entered when no tree node can be found which successfully matches the current *element* or *choice*. It moves the structural description marker backward to the left until it encounters a previously-matched *element* (in which case it pretends that this *element* did not match its tree node and starts forward again), or the (of a one-*structural-analysis* *choice* (in which case it hops to the) of the choice and starts forward), or the left-hand end of the structural description (in which case the tree is not analyzable as the structural description). As the analysis backtracks the values of the conditions of the restriction are reset to "undefined."

For certain transformations, all possible analyses of the tree are required instead of just one. In this case, after each analysis is found, the backtrack procedure is entered to find the next one, until no additional analyses can be found.

RESTRICTIONS

A restriction may be used to add conditions to a structural description or contextual feature description. Most frequently, restrictions are used to state requirements for analyzability which are otherwise inexpressible in the notation. For example, the requirement that two particular subtrees be identical can only be expressed by a restriction. If a structural description or a contextual feature description has an associated restriction, analyzability is as above, with the additional requirement that the analysis of the tree must satisfy the restriction.

A *restriction* is a Boolean combination of *conditions*, expressed using the connectives ⌐ (not), & (and), and | (or). The formal definitions are:

3.01   *restriction* ::= booleancombination[*condition*]

3.02   *condition* ::= *unary-condition* [] *binary-condition*

3.03   *unary-condition* ::= *unary-relation integer*

3.04   *binary-condition* ::= *integer binary-tree-relation node-designator* []
    integer binary-complex-relation complex-symbol-designator

3.05   *node-designator* ::= *integer* [] *node*

3.06   *complex-symbol-designator* ::= *integer* [] *complex-symbol*

If a *node-designator* is an *integer*, it refers to the tree node which matches that *integer* in the *structural-description*. For example, in the *structural-description*

% 3N S / ⟨ % (PREP) WH DEF 5N % ⟩ % # , WHERE 3 EQ 5

the *binary-condition* 3 EQ 5 requires equality of the subtrees which match the two numbered N's.

If a *complex-symbol-designator* is an *integer*, it refers to the *complex-symbol* attached to the tree node which matches the *structure* or *choice* preceded by the *integer*. Both types of *complex-symbol-designator* appear in the *structural-description*

% WH 4 (INDEF, DEF) (EVER) 6 N | * HUMAN | % #,
    WHERE ⌐ 4 INC1 | *HUMAN |

This structural description requires that the complex symbol | * HUMAN | not be included in the complex symbol of the tree node matching the choice

(INDEF, DEF). The value * means that the node matched to 4 must not be marked for the feature HUMAN.

The model incorporates most of the *conditions* which have been used in transformational grammars. It now appears that many of the conditions are made unnecessary by the additional power incorporated into the notation for the structural description; very few restrictions have been used in grammars constructed according to the model. The lists of relations are given by three final rules of the definition of restriction:

3.07   *unary-relation* ::= TRM [] NTRM [] NUL [] NNUL

3.08   *binary-tree-relation* ::= EQ [] NEQ [] DOM [] NDOM []
        DOMS [] NDOMS [] DOMBY [] NDOMBY []

3.09   *binary-complex-relation* ::= INC1 [] NINC1 [] INC2 [] NINC2 []
        CSEQ [] NCSEQ [] NDST [] NNDST [] COMP [] NCOMP

The relations are in pairs of the form **XXX** and **NXXX**, where **NXXX** is the negation of **XXX**. It is generally more efficient to use A **NXXX** B than to use ⌐ A **XXX** B, but the result is identical.

The *unary-relation* TRM requires that the match be to a terminal node of the tree. NUL requires that the match be null; it is meaningful only if the node is part of an option or choice.

The *binary-tree-relations* are equality and three dominance relations. Equality (EQ) means equality of the subtrees dominated by the matching tree nodes and includes equality of the corresponding complex symbols. For binary conditions with EQ, the *node-designator* must be an *integer*. DOM is dominance without searching below a sentence symbol, DOMS is unrestricted dominance, and DOMBY is domination by the second argument. For all three dominance conditions the *node-designator* must be a *node*. Note that A / ⟨ % B % ⟩ is exactly equivalent to 1 A, WHERE 1 DOM B. However since the model allows only one subanalysis of any element, DOM and NDOM can sometimes be used to obtain the effect of a conjunction of two subanalyses, provided one is simple. For example, 1 A / ⟨ % B C ⟩ , WHERE 1 NDOM D is impossible to express without a restriction.

We include the relation DOMBY because the structural description

3 S, WHERE 3 NDOMBY S

is the most natural way to distinguish the root S from other sentence symbols.

The *binary-complex-relations* are includes-1, includes-2, equals, is nondistinct from, and is compatible with. These are all defined in Chapter 6. Note, however, that "*m* includes *n*" is the relation "*n* is included in *m*" there defined.

STRUCTURAL CHANGE

After a successful match of the structural description to a tree, the next step in applying a transformation is to modify the tree according to the structural change. The structural change refers to the tree by the integers common to the structural description and the structural change. Subtrees have been matched to the integers by the analysis process, and these are now altered by the structural change. Thus, the effect of a transformation with *structural-description* % 2 INDEF N | −SG | %, and *structural-change* ERASE 2, is to delete the subtree which matches the *term* 2 INDEF of the *structural-description*.

The syntax rule for *transformation* is

> 8.02   *transformation* ::= TRANS *identification* .
>
> SD *structural-description* . opt[SC *structural-change*.]

The transformation just used as an example might be named PLADEL and written

> TRANS PLADEL.
>
> SD % 2 INDEF N | −SG | %.
>
> SC ERASE 2.

The identification of a transformation is discussed in the next chapter.

As a more extended example, consider the TAG transformation:

> TRANS 26 TAG.
>
> SD # NEG 3Q 4NP 5AUX VP % 7#.
>
> SC 3 ALESE 7, 4 ADLES 7, 5 ADLES 7.

The structural change for TAG is

> 3 ALESE 7, 4 ADLES 7, 5 ADLES 7

More generally, a *structural-change* is a comma list of individual *change-instructions*. The instructions are carried out in the order in which they appear in the list.

> 5.01   *structural-change* ::= clist[*change-instruction*]
>
> 5.02   *change-instruction* ::= *change* [] *conditional-change*

TAG applies to the tree

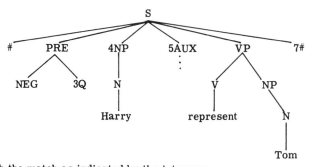

with the match as indicated by the integers.

The three change instructions of TAG adjoin subtrees as immediate left sister of the boundary symbol # and produce the tree

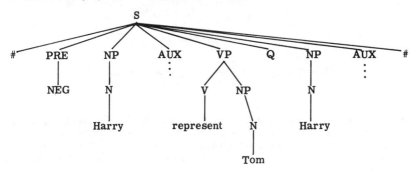

which ultimately yields the sentence

Harry doesn't represent Tom, does Harry.

The order of the instructions is important. Notice that by adding the Q, then the NP, and finally the AUX, each as immediate left sister of the boundary symbol, the order Q NP AUX is obtained. The change instructions here are all simple changes rather than conditional changes, which are discussed at the end of the chapter.

A *change* consists of an operator and one, two, or three arguments:

> 5.04   *change* ::= *unary-operator integer* []
> *tree-designator binary-tree-operator integer* []
> *complex-symbol-designator binary-complex-operator integer* []
> *complex-symbol-designator ternary-complex-operator integer*
> *integer*

Tree operators

The change operators fall into two groups: those that change tree structure and those that only alter complex symbols. The structure-changing operators are given by the rules:

> 5.06   *unary-operator* ::= ERASE [] ERASEI

> 5.07   *binary-tree-operator* ::= ADLAD [] ALADE [] ADLADI []
> ALADEI [] ADFID [] AFIDE [] ADRIA [] ARIAE [] ADRIS []
> ARISE [] ADRISI [] ARISEI [] ADLES [] ALESE [] ADLESI []
> ALESEI [] SUBST [] SUBSE [] SUBSTI [] SUBSEI []
> ADCHR [] ACHRE [] ADCHL [] ACHLE

The basic tree operations are substitution, several types of adjunction, and erasure.

The change *i* SUBST *j* substitutes a copy of subtree *i* for subtree *j*. For example, the change 4 SUBST 6 applied to the tree on the left yields the tree on the right:

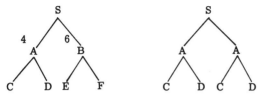

ERASE is a unary operator that deletes the indicated subtree, and then chains upward erasing all ancestors until a node with at least two daughters is encountered. Erasure always chains upward in this way, even if the erasure is given implicitly as part of an adjunction. ERASE 3 applied to the tree on the left yields the tree on the right:

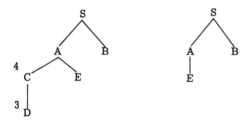

For this example, ERASE 3 and ERASE 4 have identical effects.

The names of the adjunction operators are mnemonics. For example, ADLAD is "ADd as LAst Daughter," and ALADE is "Add as LAst Daughter, with Erasure." The basic set (ADXXX) is formed using AD for "add" or "adjoin," RI, LE, FI, LA for "right," "left," "first," and "last," and finally S, D, A for "sister," "daughter," "aunt." Thus ADRIS is "ADd as RIght Sister," ADFID is "Add as FIrst Daughter". An operator in the basic set has initial AD (and no final E); it adjoins a copy of its first argument, leaving the original undisturbed. An operator with initial A (without D) and final E (AXXXE) detaches the original subtree from its former parent and adjoins it. The effect of *i* AXXXE *j* is exactly the same as that of the sequence *i* ADXXX *j*, ERASE *i*. SUBSE is likewise equivalent to substitution with erasure of the original.

The difference between the erasing and nonerasing operators is seen in the TAG example earlier, in which both ADLES and ALESE operators occur.[1] We added the erasing operators because it is more efficient to move a subtree than to make and move a copy and then erase the original.

In some grammars permutation is used, primarily in the PASSIVE transformation. Permutations are not given directly here, since only one move can be

---

[1] The reader may note that in adding *nodes* we consistently use adjunction with erasure, e.g., ES ARISE 3 instead of ES ADRIS 3. These two changes have the same effect on the tree, but because of the implementation the former is more efficient.

made at a time. However, the interchange of, say, subtrees 3 and 4 can be accomplished by the sequence 3 ADLES 4, 4 SUBSE 3, which adds a copy of 3 as the immediate left sister of 4, and then replaces the original 3 by subtree 4, at the same time erasing the original 4.

I-operators

In selecting the operators an attempt was made to be comprehensive and to include all operators that might be wanted by a user of the system. The operators just described correspond to those of the MITRE grammars. Operators ending in I are the slightly different versions which were defined for the IBM core grammar. (The ending I for the operator names is for IBM.) Basically the difference between the two sets is that the I-operations chain upward whereas the others do not.

Upward chaining of an operation is illustrated in Figure 15, which shows all four substitution operators. For the substitution *i* SUBSTI *j* both *i* and *j* chain upwards. Thus in the figure, 4 SUBSTI 5 is equivalent to 4 SUBSTI 3, and 5 SUBSTI 4 is equivalent to 3 SUBSTI 4.

The adjunction operators with names of the form ADXXXI and AXXXEI chain upward on the first operand but not on the second. Thus, 3 ADLESI 4

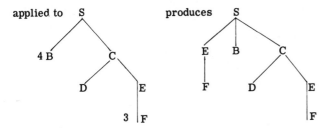

but 2 ADLESI 1 applied to

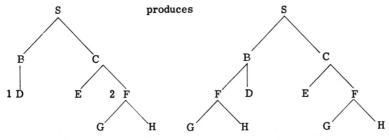

The operators ADLADI and ALADEI are defined by IBM only for adjunction to a node that does not already have daughters. *i* ADLADI *j* adds *i* as the only daughter of *j*. ADFIDI and AFIDEI do not exist since they would duplicate ADLADI and ALADEI.

The operator ERASEI is identical to ERASE and is included only so that there will be a full set of I-operators.

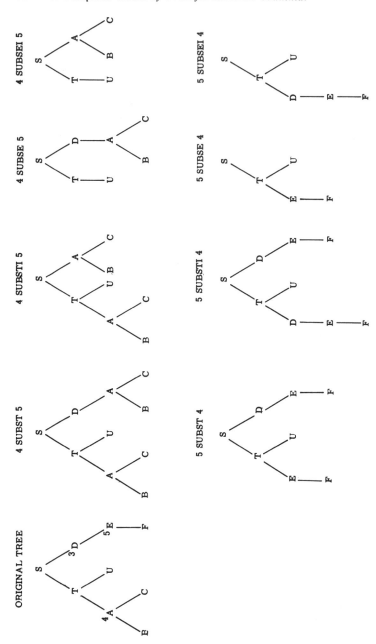

Figure 15. Substitution operators

Chomsky-adjunction

The four remaining operators are for "Chomsky-adjunction." The operators ADCHR and ACHRE Chomsky-adjoin to the right and differ by whether a new subtree is created for the adjunction or the original subtree adjoined. The left adjunctions ADCHL and ACHLE are similarly related.

In Chomsky-adjunction of node i to node j a copy of the single node j is created and inserted as the parent of j. The new node is identical to j, both in node name and complex symbol. Node i is then adjoined as sister of the original node j.

We illustrate Chomsky-adjunction in Figure 16, in the context of a complete transformational component. The figure shows transformations, a control program (identified by initial CP), and the application of the transformations to a particular tree.

In Chapter 9 we discuss control programs fully. The one in the example is particularly simple, merely specifying that the transformations are to be applied in order, and that the tree is to be output after each transformation.

We now follow the application of the transformations one by one.

The structural description of T1 matches nodes 2 and 5. A copy of the subtree headed by node 2 is to be Chomsky-adjoined to the right of node 5. Node 8 heads a new subtree which is a copy of the subtree of node 2. The new node 7 is the parent of both node 5 and node 8. Node 8 has been Chomsky-adjoined to the right of node 5; it is now the right sister of node 5.

Transformation T2 adds a complex symbol to node 8. T3 matches nodes 3, 7, and 8. A copy of 3 is Chomsky-adjoined to the left of 8. As a result the new node 12 appears as left sister of node 8. The new node 11, which has been created as parent of 12 and 8, has the same name and the same complex symbol as node 8.

Transformation T4 illustrates both operators for Chomsky-adjunction with erasure.

Chomsky-adjunction is the only change that automatically attaches complex symbols to nodes that dominate other non-terminal nodes. The MERGEF and MOVEF operators may be used to put complex symbols at any position in the tree, but normally are used for nodes that dominate only terminal nodes.

EXAMPLE

The following example[2] from the morphology of French verbs shows that Chomsky-adjunction, with its automatic complex symbol transfer, provides a simple method for the adjunction of auxiliaries, when the tense marker is carried as a feature of the verb. The morphological derivation of the verb

> MANGE | +V +VE + PASSIF *PASSE *FUTUR *INF *PERS
> *DEUXPERS *FEM *PLUR |

requires the following operations:

> (1) adjoin the auxiliary *est* at the left of *mange*

---

[2] Due to Yves Ch. Morin.

"EXAMPLES OF CHOMSKY ADJUNCTION"

TRANSFORMATIONS

TRANS T1.   SD 4 A 9 E.
             SC 4 ADCHR 9.

TRANS T2.   SD % E 1 A %.
             SC | +K | MERGEF 1.

TRANS T3.   SD 1 B % E 2 A.
             SC 1 ADCHL 2.

TRANS T4.   SD B 1 C 2 F 3 B % 4 C.
             SC 2 ACHRE 1, 4 ACHLE 3.

"CONTROL" CP T1; TREE; T2; TREE; T3; TREE; T4.

    $END "END OF TRANSFORMATIONS"

INPUT TREE

```
1 S    2 A    3 B
              4 C
       5 E    6 F
```

TREE AFTER T1

```
1 S    2 A    3 B
              4 C
       7 E    5 E    6 F
              8 A    9 B
                    10 C
```

TREE AFTER T2

```
1 S    2 A    3 B
              4 C
       7 E    5 E    6 F
              8 A    9 B
                    10 C
```

NODE 8 A
     | +K |

TREE AFTER T3

```
1 S    2 A    3 B
              4 C
       7 E    5 E    6 F
             11 A   12 B
                     8 A    9 B
                           10 C
```

NODE 11 A
     | +K |
NODE 8 A
     | +K |

TREE AFTER T4

```
1 S    2 A    3 B
             13 C    4 C
                     6 F
       7 E   11 A   14 B   10 C
                    12 B
                     8 A    9 B
```

NODE 11 A
     | +K |
NODE 8 A
          | +K | Figure 16. Chomsky-adjunction
```
```

(2) adjoin the morpheme *-é* at the right of *mange*

(3) transfer the features of *mange* to *est*

(4) delete all features of *mange* with the exception of | *FEM *PLUR |.

Operations (3) and (4) are necessary, because after the auxiliary is introduced it takes the tense and person morphemes, while the past participle loses its verbal properties and becomes regular with respect to gender and number. For example,

Les carottes ont été mangées.—"The carrots had been eaten."

By using Chomsky-adjunction for operation (1), operation (3) is carried out automatically, and the four operations can be accomplished by a single transformation:

TRANS PASSIF.

SD % 1 V | +PASSIF | % .

SC | +PASSIF | ERASEF 1 , EST ACHLE 1 ,

   | *FEM *PLUR | SAVEF 1 , E ALADE 1 .

The effect of the transformation is shown by

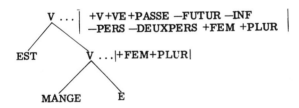

V ... | +V +VE +PASSIF +PASSE —FUTUR —INF |
       | —PERS —DEUXPERS + FEM + PLUR |

MANGE

which becomes

V ... | +V+VE+PASSE —FUTUR —INF |
       | —PERS —DEUXPERS +FEM +PLUR |

EST   V ...|+FEM+PLUR|

MANGE   E

The convention for interpreting complex symbols on nodes that have both terminal and non-terminal daughters must be that the complex symbol applies to the terminal nodes only. (This convention is not implicit in the model, but can be adopted by writing only transformations that adhere to it.) The morphological rules for gender and number apply only to nodes not marked +VE. They adjoin the feminine morpheme (EE) and the plural morpheme (ES) to nodes which are marked +FEM and +PLUR respectively. This application gives the expected result for the number and gender agreement of the past participle:

V ... |+FEM+PLUR|

MANGE   E

becomes

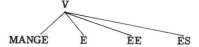

These rules do not apply to EST because the feature specification +VE indicates a verbal morphology, in which the specifications +FEM and +PLUR do not lead to the usual feminine and plural morphemes.

Tree designators

In the examples so far the arguments for the tree operators have been integers indicating subtrees matched by the analysis process. However, the first argument of a binary tree operator may also be either a *tree* within parentheses or a *node*.

    5.05   *tree-designator* ::= (*tree*) [] *node* [] *integer*

An example of a transformation that adds subtrees which are *nodes* is PASSIVE, which exchanges subject and agent and adds BE EN. A use of (*tree*) as *tree-designator* is (A⟨B | +E | C ⟩) SUBST 3 which changes

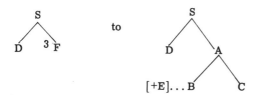

A *node* with *complex-symbol*, like N | +ANIMATE |, is not a *tree-designator*. However, it is a *tree*, so (N | +ANIMATE |) is a *tree-designator* and hence (N | +ANIMATE |) ALESE 3 is a *change*.

Null arguments

An *integer* used as an argument in a *change* will fail to designate anything if the corresponding *term* of the *structural-description* is not matched. Changes with null arguments are ignored. For example, an analysis for the transformation REL3 need not match the term 2(PREP). If it does not, the instruction 2 ARISE 1 is ignored.

    TRANS REL3.

    SD 1# % S ⟨ % 2 (PREP) 3NP ⟨ (DET) 4REL N (S) ⟩ % ⟩ % .

    SC TH3 ALADE 4 , 3 ARISE 1 , 2 ARISE 1.

Complex symbol operators

There are three binary operators and one ternary operator for complex symbols:

5. 08   *binary-complex-operator* ::= ERASEF [] MERGEF [] SAVEF []

5. 09   *ternary-complex-operator* ::= MOVEF

These changes are defined in Chapter 6. As examples, the agreement transformation AG uses MOVEF to mark the PRES or PAST node with either +SG or —SG so as to match the feature specification of the subject; TSUBJ uses MERGEF to mark as +NOM the first noun of the first noun phrase.

TRANS 13 AG.

SD # (PRE) NP ⟨ (DET) 3N | *SG | % ⟩ 4 (PRES , PAST) % # .

SC | *SG | MOVEF 3 4.

TRANS TSUBJ AC .

SD # (PRE) NP ⟨ % 1N % ⟩ .

SC | +NOM | MERGEF 1.

The *complex-symbol-designator* may be a *complex-symbol* as above, or, like the *tree-designator*, it may be an *integer*.

3. 06   *complex-symbol-designator* ::= *complex-symbol* [] *integer*

An *integer* here points to the complex symbol of the matching tree node. For example, 3 SAVEF 4 would reduce the complex symbol of node 4 by deleting all feature specifications except those also in the complex symbol of node 3.

Conditional change

In addition to the simple changes discussed previously, the model also allows conditional change:

5. 03   *conditional-change* ::= IF ⟨ *restriction* ⟩ THEN
             ⟨ *structural-change* ⟩ opt[ELSE ⟨ *structural-change* ⟩]

The *structural-change* following THEN is performed if the *restriction* is met; otherwise, the *structural-change* following ELSE is performed, or, if none is given, no change is made. The conditional change can make one transformation do the work of two.

For example, in the transformation CP1 the conditional change allows a feature value to determine which of two new nodes is added:

TRANS "COMPLEMENTIZER PLACEMENT 1" .

SD # % 3N | *C | S / ⟨ 4NP (T , BE , HAVE , V) % ⟩ % # .

SC IF ⟨ 3 INC1 | +C | ⟩ THEN ⟨ CPLUS ALESEI 4 ⟩
                    ELSE ⟨ CMINUS ALESEI 4 ⟩ .

CP1 matches a tree only if the tree node matching 3 includes-1 | *C |, i.e., is specified for C. If the value of C is +, a node CPLUS is adjoined; if the value is −, CMINUS is adjoined.

Morphological rules, which add endings based on combinations of feature specifications, can best be expressed by the use of the conditional change. For example, a first approximation to a verb agreement system might be:

TRANS 2 ADDVAGR.

SD # % 1V | −PERS −PERS2 *PLUR *CONJ | % # .

SC IF ⟨ 1 INC1 | −PLUR | ⟩

    THEN ⟨ IF ⟨ 1 INC1 | −CONJ | ⟩ THEN ⟨ T ALADE 1 ⟩

    ELSE ⟨ IT ALADE 1 ⟩ ⟩

    ELSE ⟨ IF ⟨ 1 INC1 | −CONJ | ⟩ THEN ⟨ NT ALADE 1 ⟩

    ELSE ⟨ UNT ALADE 1 ⟩ ⟩

ADDVAGR applies to nodes V with complex symbols that include −PERS and −PERS2. It can be summarized as:

In presence of	Add
−PLUR −CONJ	T
−PLUR +CONJ	IT
+PLUR −CONJ	NT
+PLUR −CONJ	UNT

If all verbs (V) are marked for PLUR and CONJ, the specifications *PLUR and *CONJ can be dropped from the structural description.

Order of change

The left-to-right order of the change instructions in the structural change defines the order of their execution. Particular attention to ordering is required when making several adjunctions to the same node, or when making deletions.

The TAG example given earlier shows that left-sister adjunction preserves order. Right-sister adjunction reverses order: A ARISE 1, B ARISE 1, C ARISE 1 adds each new node as the *immediate* right sister of the node designated by 1, with the result C B A. Last-daughter adjunction preserves order and first-daughter adjunction reverses it.

Erasure or any adjunction with erasure destroys tree nodes. Any subsequent reference to the deleted nodes is meaningless. The structural change ERASE 2, 2 ADLAD 1 is not well-defined, nor are ERASE 2, | *SG | MOVEF 2 1 and 2 ALESE 3, 2 ARISE 4.

Tree-pruning

Ross (1966) introduces the operation of "tree-pruning," which deletes an intermediate node. It is usually suggested for nodes with only one daughter, and for specific nodes only. Tree-pruning differs from the other deletion operations, which delete a node and its subtree; tree-pruning deletes an intermediate node

and reattaches its daughter(s). Pruning an S from the tree on the left produces
the tree on the right:

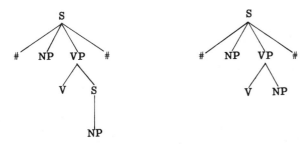

Tree-pruning can be thought of as a transformation that must be applied whenever its structural description is met. It thus fails to occupy a fixed place in a
linear ordering of transformations. The system of Gross (1968) has an instruction by which the user gives a list of nodes for which pruning is to apply, and
the operation then takes place whenever applicable. We do not have any explicit
treatment of tree-pruning in our model, although a user may simulate the
convention by writing appropriate transformations. For example, the grammar
of Nagara and Smith (1970) tree-prunes in the transformations PRUNE and
NIEXT:

    TRANS 41 PRUNE "S PRUNING" I OB AC (S) .

        SD # % 1S ⟨ 2NP ⟩ % # .

        SC 2 SUBSE 1 .

    TRANS 13 NIEXT "NP-NI EXTRACTION" I OB AC (S) .

        SD # % 1NP 2S ⟨ 3NP ⟨ % NI ⟩ 4 (NP) 5 (NP , S) 6 (V) ⟩ % # .

        SC 3 ARISE 1 , IF ⟨ NUL 6 ⟩ THEN ⟨ 4 ALESE 2 , 5 ARISE 2 ⟩ .

In this grammar an embedded S in pruned unless it dominates a verb. PRUNE
simply prunes an S that immediately dominates only an NP; it would apply in
the example given. NIEXT combines pruning with a transformation that can
produce a tree in need of pruning. NIEXT first extracts an NP from an
embedded S. If there is no verb in that S, the remaining daughters are moved
out. Pruning occurs because the S is automatically erased as its last daughter
is moved.

CHAPTER 9

The Transformational Component

The transformational component of a grammar consists primarily of a set of transformations; but it must also contain what Fillmore (1963) has called "traffic rules" that specify the order in which the transformations are applied. These rules may be considered either as part of linguistic theory, in which case one set of rules applies to all grammars, or as an explicit part of a grammar. In this work we take the position that the traffic rules, or "control program," are given in the transformational component of a grammar. We do not wish to maintain anything at all about the possibility that a universal set of traffic rules will someday be found, but at the present time linguists disagree on what the traffic rules are. We therefore define a language in which the user can formulate traffic rules.

The suggestion that the metatheory of grammar contains some complex scheme for traffic laws within a grammar and a control unit which directs the order of application of rules occurs in Lees (1960) as one of three alternative plans for rule ordering. The language defined in this chapter may be viewed as a proposal for Lees's "complex scheme."

The control language enables the user to:

1. Group transformations into ordered sets and apply transformations either individually or by transformation set.

2. Specify the order in which the transformation sets are to be considered.

3. Specify the subtrees in which a transformation set is to be applied.

4. Allow the order of application to depend on which transformations have previously modified the tree.

5. Apply a transformation set either once or repeatedly.

The control language takes advantage of mechanisms that must already be in any system of transformational grammar. For example, the "IN-instruction," used to determine the subtree for which a transformation is to be invoked, itself uses a transformation in this determination. Likewise, there is no provision for placing special indices on the sentence tree, but instead feature specifications, already in the system, are used. The decision to stay within the devices already available causes some difficulty in expressing some proposed cycling orders, as is apparent in some of the examples. However, the alternative is to include special devices specific to the various proposals in the literature, which is undesirable unless some general ideas can be abstracted from them.

The purpose of the control program is to determine in what order in the derivation and at what point in the tree a transformation is invoked. Thus, in the familiar control sequence, "apply the cyclic transformations to the lowest sentence," the control program must select the lowest sentence subtree and then invoke the transformations in order for that subtree.

In this chapter we discuss the transformational component in relation to the control program, then explain how a transformation is invoked and what role its parameters play. Then we turn to the control language itself and show how it provides a step-by-step selection both of the transformation to be invoked and of the tree node that is the top node for the analysis algorithm.

TRANSFORMATIONS

The transformational component, *transformations,* consists of a list of trans-formations and a control program:

8. 01   *transformations* ::= TRANSFORMATIONS list[*transformation*]
CP *control-program* . $

A dollar sign terminates this component, as it does *phrase-structure* and *lexicon.* The delimiters for the *control-program* are the CP and the period.

A transformation has three parts:

8. 02   *transformation* ::= TRANS *identification* .
SD *structural-description* . opt[SC *structural-change*.]

Each part is preceded by an identifier and followed by a period. A *trans-formation* without *structural-change* merely defines a match of *structural-description* and *tree;* the *IN-instruction* of the control language uses such transformations.

Example

```
TRANS 7 PASSIVE "PASSIVE" I OB AACC ( P ) .
    SD # ( PRE ) 3NP AUX ( HAVE EN ) ( BE ING ) 5V ( PREP ) 7NP %
       PREP 10P % # , WHERE ¬3 EQ 7.
    SC 3 SUBSTI 10, 7 SUBSEI 3, BE ALESEI 5, EN ALESEI 5.
```

The first line contains *identification,* the next two give a *structural-description,* and the last has a *structural-change.*

The *identification* of a transformation can have four parts, but only a name is required:

8. 03   *identification* ::= opt[*integer*] *transformation-name*
opt[list[*parameter*]] opt[*keywords*]

8. 04   *transformation-name* ::= *word*

The *integer* serves only for external identification; within a grammar trans-formations are always referred to by their *transformation-name*s. In the example, the *integer* 7 is the user's reference, PASSIVE is the internal name, and "PASSIVE" is a comment.

A *parameter* of a transformation provides information to be used in the control program; each is of one of three types:

> 8. 05   *parameter* ::= *group-number* [] *optionality* [] *repetition*

By means of *group-numbers*,

> 8. 06   *group-number* ::= I [] II [] III [] IV [] V [] VI [] VII

the user can create subsets of transformations for convenience in writing his control program. Particular *group-numbers* have no *a priori* meaning; they acquire meaning from their use in the *control-program*. If no group number is specified, a transformation automatically receives the same group number as the preceding transformation (or I for the first transformation).

Optionality and *repetition* are the topic of the next section; then *keywords* are discussed.

INVOKING A TRANSFORMATION

We use the phrase "invoke a transformation" to mean the process that begins when the control program starts to consider a transformation, and ends when the control program is ready to turn to the next transformation or instruction. To say that a transformation has been invoked does not necessarily mean that its structural change has been applied, or even that the analysis process has been tried: the invocation may end on a failure of the analysis process, or on a negative decision for an option.

In invoking a transformation, we must consider whether or not it is optional, whether and in what way it is to be repeated, and which subtrees are to be analyzed. A standard convention, described later, decides what subtrees to use; explicit instructions in the control program may override this convention. We postpone the discussion of what subtree to use, and describe invocation of a transformation for a specified subtree.

Optionality and repetition

Whether a transformation is obligatory or optional is specified by a parameter:

> 8. 07   *optionality* ::= OB [] OP

Each transformation must be either obligatory or optional. Transformations that operate as though conditionally optional must be broken into two. If no *optionality* is specified, a transformation is obligatory.

Whether a transformation is repeated, and if so, how analysis and change alternate, is specified by the repetition parameter:

> 8. 08   *repetition* ::= AC [] ACAC [] AACC [] AAC

A and C abbreviate "analysis" and "change"; we use these mnemonics to avoid terms like "cyclic," "iterative," and "recursive," which already have several interpretations. If no repetition is specified, a transformation is AC.

The two possibilities for optionality interact with the four modes of repetition to give eight distinct sequences of action for invoking a transformation for a specified subtree. Table 1 summarizes the four repetition cases for optional transformations. Omitting the step numbered 0 gives the corresponding obligatory case. (The phrase "take the next" means "take the first," if none has previously been taken.)

TABLE 1

Invoking a Transformation

For an OPTIONAL transformation, do all steps.

For an OBLIGATORY transformation, omit step 0.

Repetition	Action Sequence
AC	0. OPTIONS: CONTINUE or STOP 1. Find first match; if none, STOP 2. Structural change 3. STOP
ACAC	0. OPTIONS: CONTINUE or STOP 1. Find first match; if none, STOP 2. Structural change 3. GO TO 0
AACC	1. Find all matches; if none, STOP 2. Take next match; if none, STOP 0. OPTIONS: CONTINUE or GO TO 2 3. Structural change 4. GO TO 2
AAC	0. OPTIONS: CONTINUE or STOP 1. Find all matches; if none, STOP 2. Take one match at random 3. Structural change 4. STOP

The simplest case is AC-OB. The analysis algorithm attempts to match the structural description to the subtree. As soon as one match is found, analysis terminates, and the structural change applies. The process terminates if no match is found, or after the modification of the tree.

The optional case AC-OP differs in that an initial decision determines whether to continue as in the obligatory case or stop. In our implementation, which operates in a computer system without user interaction, options are chosen at random. In an implementation of the same control language in an interactive environment, these choices could be made by the user from his console.

In the ACAC cases, analysis and change alternate. Essentially, the transformation applies again to its own output. The analysis algorithm always finds the first match, but, after change, this should not be the same match as before.

The user must exercise care to avoid infinite repetition of ACAC transformations.

In the AACC and AAC cases, the analysis algorithm applies only once: it returns all possible matches. Then, for AACC all corresponding changes are made; for AAC one match is selected at random and the corresponding change is made.

The first three repetition modes are found in the literature under other names. The case AAC is new and is suggested by difficulties found in grammars run on the computer system.

The repetition AAC

Consider the WH-Attraction transformation of Rosenbaum and Lochak (1966):

10	WHA	WH-Attraction					OB		

$$\# \quad U \quad ART \quad [\, NP \; W \; \begin{Bmatrix} PREP + [\, WH \; X \,]_{NP} \\ [\, WH \; X \,]_{NP} \end{Bmatrix} Y \,]_S \; Z \quad \#$$

1	2	3	4	5	6	7	8	9	
1	2	3	6 + 4	5	$\emptyset$	7	8	9	$\Longrightarrow$

In our notation, this transformation is:

TRANS 10 WHA "WHA-ATTRACTION" I OB AAC.

    SD # % ART S / ⟨ 4NP % 6 (* ⟨ PREP NP / ⟨ WH % ⟩ ⟩,

    NP / ⟨ WH % ⟩) % ⟩ % # .

    SC 6 ALESEI 4.

The structural description contains a choice between PREP NP and NP; but any tree which matches the first possibility also matches the other. The intention is that if both can be matched, either analysis can be used. However, any analysis algorithm must have an order of search which either always selects PREP NP or always selects NP alone. The AAC parameter allows the analysis algorithm to find both, and then selects one at random.

The case AAC is also useful for the WH-question transformation of a grammar of Old English (Traugott, 1967). There the problem is more difficult, since more than one element at a time may be questioned. The following transformations together have the desired effect.

TRANS WHA1 "WH-QUESTION" AACC OP.

    SD % 1 Q % 2 NP %.

    SC WH ALESE 2, ERASE 1.

TRANS WHA2 "WH-QUESTION" AAC OB.

    SD % 1 Q % 2 NP %.

    SC WH ALESE 2, ERASE 1.

WHA1 optionally inserts WH as left sister of zero or more NP's in the sentence. If at least one WH is inserted, the Q is erased and WHA2 fails. If no WH is inserted by WHA1, the OB transformation WHA2 inserts exactly one WH as left sister of a randomly selected NP.

Keywords

The optional list of keywords,

> 8.09   *keywords* ::= (list[*node*])

is a technical device to bypass application of the analysis algorithm. The top node for an analysis must dominate all of the keywords (with or without an intervening S); if not, the analysis is assumed to have been tried and to have failed.

For example, a good set of keywords for the transformation WHA above would be (WH S) . Analysis of a subtree would take place only if it contained both WH and S. The top node of the subtree must dominate the keyword; it does not itself count as the keyword. Thus, the keyword S is not automatically satisfied, but assures an embedded S in the subtree.

This completes the discussion of how the model invokes a transformation for a specified top node. Before we turn to the selection of transformations and the specification of the top node, that is, the interpretation of the control program, we digress to consider rule features.

Simulation of rule features

Lakoff (1965) proposes rule features to help determine whether to invoke a transformation. He classifies transformations as major and minor. For each transformation and tree, a particular item in the tree "governs" the trans-formation. A major transformation is invoked unless the governing tree node is negatively specified for the rule feature; a minor rule is invoked only if it is positively specified. Since there is no well-defined way to locate the tree node that governs a transformation, we simulate the effect of rule features by the use of inherent features.

As an example, consider the transformation TRINF:

TRANS 506 TRINF (S).

SD # % 4V | +TRINF | 5(SN) S / ⟨ 7QUE (PRE) 8SN 9(V, ADJ) % ⟩

11(SN) % #, WHERE 5 EQ 8 | 8 EQ 11.

SC | +INF | MERGEF 9, ERASE 7, ERASE 8.

In the lexicon the feature TRINF indicates which verbs must, may, and cannot undergo the transformation TRINF. Verbs with the feature specification +TRINF must undergo the transformation, those with the specification —TRINF (or no specification) must not undergo it, and verbs marked *TRINF optionally undergo it. TRINF is a minor rule. If the complex symbol +TRINF is deleted from its structural description, and the restriction 4 NINC1 | —TRINF | is added, it becomes a major rule.

CONTROL PROGRAMS

Basically, a *control-program* is a semicolon list of *instructions*:

    9.01'   *control-program* ::= sclist[*instruction*]

(This is a shortened version of rule 9.01, given in full later.)

Separation of *instructions* by semicolons follows a common practice in programming languages. The instructions are executed in the order given, unless the program itself indicates otherwise.

The definition of *instruction* is recursive; a semicolon list of instructions enclosed in angular brackets is also an *instruction*.

    9.03   *instruction* ::=
            transformation-element [] *control-element* []
            ⟨ sclist [*instruction*] ⟩

    9.04   *transformation-element* ::=
            transformation-name [] *group-number*

*Transformation-element*s are the simplest instructions. We discuss them first, and then return to *control-element*.

If a control program[1] consists only of a transformation name, as in

    CP TRAN1 .   (1)

it invokes that transformation and stops. If a sequence of transformation names is given,

    CP PASSIVE; FLIP; REGDEL .   (2)

the program invokes each transformation and then proceeds to the next. A standard procedure selects the subtrees for which each transformation is invoked.

Subtree selection

The standard procedure for selecting subtrees for analysis applies unless IN-instructions override it. The procedure selects each S in the tree in turn as the top node of a subtree for analysis. The steps for each transformation are:

    1.   List all the S's in the tree. If none, STOP.

    2.   Take from the list the next S that dominates all the keywords. If none, STOP.

    3.   Invoke the transformation for this S.

    4.   GO TO 2.

---

[1] The examples show *control-program*s between CP and a period, although these delimiters are a part of the format *transformations*, not the format *control-program*.

The order of the S's in the list is arbitrary; the standard procedure should be used only if order is immaterial. No S is added to the list after step 1. At step 3 the appropriate case of Table 1 is carried out.

Control program (2) calls for this standard subtree selection. Thus, if there are two sentence symbols S_1 and S_2, the order is:

> Invoke PASSIVE at S_1
>
> Invoke PASSIVE at S_2
>
> Invoke FLIP at S_1
>
> Invoke FLIP at S_2
>
> Invoke REGDEL at S_1
>
> Invoke REGDEL at S_2

If the transformations of (2) have the same group number, say II, and are the only transformations of that group, then the program

$$\text{CP II.} \tag{3}$$

has exactly the same effect as (2).

The power of the control program comes from a set of *control-elements*:

> 9.05   *control-element* ::= *IN-instruction* [] *RPT-instruction* []
> *IF-instruction* [] *FLAG-instruction* [] *GOTO-instruction* []
> *TRACE-instruction* [] *STOP-instruction*

The IN-instruction alone gives us enough power to express the most common cycling patterns. We follow its explanation with three major examples and then explain the other control elements.

IN-INSTRUCTIONS

In most grammars, groups of transformations must be invoked for a single sentence subtree before the next subtree is considered. Often they are invoked for subtrees with special characteristics, such as lowest sentence, next-to-lowest sentence, or top sentence. The IN-instruction gives the control language the capability of expressing these requirements.

> 9.06   *IN-instruction* ::=
>   IN *transformation-name* (*integer*) DO ⟨ *control-program* ⟩

The *transformation-name* here is the name of some transformation in the grammar. It need not have a structural change and should belong to a group that is never invoked.

The IN-instruction uses a transformation to select the subtrees for which to invoke a subprogram. The prototype of the IN-instruction is

IN LOWESTS (2) DO ⟨ II ⟩   (4)

LOWESTS is an ordinary transformation. Its structural description contains a *term* with *integer* 2 that matches a "lowest sentence." The IN-instruction (4) works as follows: LOWESTS is invoked. If the analysis succeeds, the structural change, if any, is applied. The tree node matched to *term* 2 becomes the current lowest sentence, and each transformation of group II is invoked for it. Then LOWESTS is again invoked to search for another lowest sentence. The instruction terminates when no new lowest sentence is found.

We give a step-by-step description of the execution of (4), comparing the process with the standard procedure used for (3).

The reader may find the examples more helpful than the full details.

The procedure for (3) takes a transformation and applies it to all S's. Then it takes the next transformation. The steps are:

1.   Take the next transformation of II. If none, STOP.

2.   List all S's. If none, STOP.

3.   Take next S. If none, GO TO 1.

4.   Invoke the transformation for this S.

5.   GO TO 3.

The procedure for (4) selects a qualified S and does all transformations for that S only. Then it selects another qualified S. The steps are:

1.   List all S's. If none, STOP.

2.   Take next S. If none, GO TO 5.

3.1 Invoke LOWESTS for this S. If unsuccessful, GO TO 2.

3.2 If the tree node matched to term 2 is not new, GO TO 2.

4.1 Take the next transformation of group II. If none, GO TO 2.

4.2 Invoke it for the subtree found in step 3.

4.3 GO TO 4.1.

5.   If step 4 has been reached since last time at this step, GO TO 1.

6.   STOP.

Notice that group II transformations may change the tree so that analysis for LOWESTS succeeds where it previously failed.

The IN-instructions give programs (5) and (6) very different effects.

CP IN NEXT(1) DO ⟨ TRAN2; TRAN3; TRAN4 ⟩ .   (5)

CP IN NEXT(1) DO 〈 TRAN2 〉 ;
   IN NEXT(1) DO 〈 TRAN3 〉 ;
   IN NEXT(1) DO 〈 TRAN4 〉 .
(6)

In program (5) the subtree found by NEXT is used for all three transformations, before going on to the next subtree. In (6) each transformation is done for all subtrees found by NEXT, before going on to the next transformation. In (5) all three transformations are invoked for each subtree found by NEXT, even if after TRAN2, say, the structural description of NEXT is no longer satisfied. In (6) the structural description of NEXT is verified before each invocation of a transformation.

The *control-program* within an *IN-instruction* may be more complex. For example, the program

CP IN LOWESTS(3) DO 〈 I; TREE 〉 ; II.

executes the instruction TREE, which outputs the tree, after each complete invocation of group I. Later we give an example in which one *IN-instruction* contains another.

The subtree selected by the IN-instruction need not have S as its root. Some recent developments suggest that it may be desirable to use noun-phrase subtrees for some transformations (see Chomsky, forthcoming).

THREE BOTTOM-TO-TOP CYCLES

With the instructions already introduced we can construct control programs that correspond to the most usual general suggestion for traffic rules, namely, a bottom-to-top cycle. The examples differ in the way they achieve the cycle.

Example 1—Boundary erasure before embedding

The Core grammar contains two groups of transformations—cyclic and post-cyclic. The cyclic rules apply to a "lowest sentence," which is an S analyzable as # % #, where the skip % does not have any boundary symbol # in its range. A final transformation at the end of a cycle erases the boundaries of the currently lowest sentence, and the sentence next above it becomes lowest. When the cyclic rules have finally applied to the topmost sentence, the postcyclic rules apply. We repeat in our format an example from Rosenbaum and Lochak (1966).

Figure 17 contains the transformational component. The transformation LOWESTS selects the lowest sentence for which the boundaries have not been erased. The transformations also include a cyclic transformation TA that deletes a suitably located A, a cyclic transformation TB that erases sentence boundaries, and a postcyclic transformation TC that deletes any C. The phrase "cyclic" and "postcyclic" are informal and are only comments. The two groups are formally identified by the group numbers I and II.

TRANSFORMATIONS

    TRANS LOWESTS III.

    SD 1 S ⌐ / ⟨ % S ⟨ # % # ⟩ % ⟩ , WHERE 1 DOM # .

"CYCLIC TRANSFORMATIONS"

    TRANS TA I.

    SD # 2 A % # .

    SC ERASE 2.

    TRANS TB I.

    SD 1 # % 3 # .

    SC ERASE 1, ERASE 3.

"POST-CYCLIC TRANSFORMATION"

    TRANS TC II.

    SD % 2 C %.

    SC ERASE 2.

CP "CONTROL PROGRAM"

    IN LOWESTS (1) DO ⟨ I ⟩ ; II.

$END "END OF TRANSFORMATIONS"

Figure 17. Transformational component of example 1

We use tree (7) to illustrate the execution of the control program.

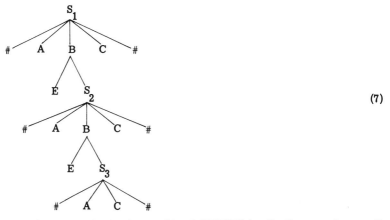

(7)

The control program begins by invoking LOWESTS for the three sentences: S_1, S_2, and S_3. Subtrees S_1 and S_2 fail to yield a successful match, but S_3 qualifies as a lowest sentence. Group II, consisting of TA and TB, is then invoked with S_3 as top node. TA deletes the A of the lowest sentence, and TB deletes the boundaries giving the result (8).

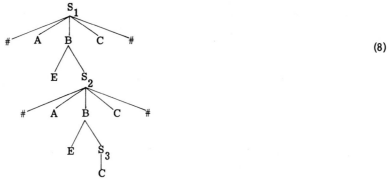

(8)

LOWESTS is then invoked again for S_1 which again fails and then for S_2 which this time is successfully analyzed as a lowest S. Transformation TA deletes an A; transformation TB then deletes boundaries to produce (9).

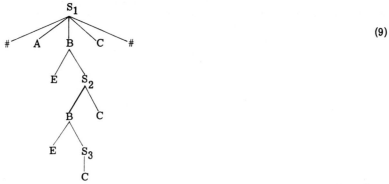

(9)

LOWESTS is again invoked for S_3 and fails. It is invoked again for S_1 and succeeds because S_1 is now the lowest S. Transformation TA deletes the remaining A and transformation TB produces (10).

(10)

This application of the rules leaves a tree for which LOWESTS fails for all three S's. The control program then proceeds to the next instruction, which is the group number II. There is only one transformation, TC, in the group; it produces the final result (11).

(11)

Example 2—Boundary erasure during embedding

Example 1 uses the fact that boundary symbols are erased at the end of the transformations of group I and before the sentence is embedded. In some grammars, boundary symbols are not erased at the end of a group, but are erased as the sentences are embedded. The grammar of Figure 18 contains auxiliary transformations and a control program that give a bottom-to-top cycle in this case.

```
TRANSFORMATIONS

    "THESE ARE USED TO TEST THE CONTROL PROGRAM"

        TRANS ADDA I. SD # 1N %. SC A ALADE 1.
        TRANS EMBED II AACC.
        SD S/<% S/<1# % 2#> %> .
        SC ERASE 1, ERASE 2.


    "TRANSFORMATIONS FOR THE CONTROL PROGRAM"

        TRANS BOTTOM IV (#).
        SD 1S¬/<% S %> .
        TRANS ONEUP IV (S #).
        SD 1S/<% S<# % #> %> .
        TRANS ONEDOWN IV (# S).
        SD 1S¬/<% S/<% S<# % #> %> %>.

    "CONTROL PROGRAM" CP  IN BOTTOM(1) DO <I>;
        IN ONEDOWN(1) DO <IN ONEUP(1) DO <II;I>> .
    $ENDTRA
```

Figure 18. Grammar of example 2

The transformation ONEDOWN selects a sentence symbol that does not dominate an S that in turn dominates an S with boundaries, that is, it selects an S that is not too high in the tree. ONEUP, on the other hand, selects an S that dominates an S with boundaries, that is, an S that is at least high enough. The double use of the IN-instruction has the effect of combining the two structural descriptions, so that an S is selected at exactly the right height in the tree. The application of the control program is illustrated by giving the order of the steps in the transformation of Figure 19 to Figure 20.

```
TEST FOR KEN'S CONTROL PROGRAM
  1 S          2 #
               3 N
               4 S          5 #
                            6 N
                            7 S          8 #
                                         9 N
                                        10 S         11 #
                                                     12 N
                                                     13 #
                                        14 #
                            15 S        16 #
                                        17 N
                                        18 #
                            19 #
               20 S         21 #
                            22 N
                            23 #
               24 #

          #N#N#N#N###N###N##
```

Figure 19. Base tree

```
TEST FOR KEN'S CONTROL PROGRAM
  1 S          2 #
               3 N         30 A
               4 S          6 N        29 A
                            7 S         9 N        28 A
                                       10 S        12 N        25 A
                            15 S       17 N        26 A
               20 S         22 N       27 A
               24 #

          #A A A A A A#
```

Figure 20. Surface tree

The transformations apply as follows:

BOTTOM selects 10: S
    ADDA adds A to 12: N
BOTTOM selects 15: S
    ADDA adds A to 17: N
BOTTOM selects 20: S
    ADDA adds A to 22: N
No additional S's satisfy BOTTOM.
ONEDOWN selects 7: S
    ONEUP accepts 7: S
        EMBED erases 11: # and 13: #
        ADDA adds A to 9: N

ONEDOWN selects 4: S
 ONEUP accepts 4: S
  EMBED erases 8: #, 14: #, 16: #, and 18: #
  ADDA adds A to 6: N
ONEDOWN selects 1: S
 ONEUP accepts 1: S
  EMBED erases 5: #, 19: #, 21: #, and 23: #
  ADDA adds A to 3: N
No additional S's satisfy ONEDOWN.

A control program that at first might appear to accomplish the same purpose as the previous one uses only two control transformations:

```
"CONTROL PROGRAM TRANSFORMATIONS"

TRANS BOTTOM IV (#).
SD 1S¬/<% S %> .

TRANS NEXTS IV (S #) .
SD 1S/<% 2S¬/<% S<# % #> %> %>, WHERE 2 DOM # .


CP: "CONTROL PROGRAM"
  IN BOTTOM(1) DO <I>;
  IN NEXTS(1) DO <II;I>;
  III.
```

For trees of depth two, this control program is equivalent to the previous one. For the general case it is not equivalent, as we see by applying it to the same test tree. At first it is identical with the other and adds A to nodes 12, 17 and 22. However, it then does the following:

NEXTS selects 1: S
 EMBED erases 5: #, 19: #, 21: #, 23: #
 ADDA adds A to 3: N
NEXTS selects 4: S
 EMBED erases 8: #, 14: #, 16: #, 18: #
NEXTS selects 7: S
 EMBED erases 11: # and 13: #

The final result is the tree of Figure 21.

```
TEST FOR KEN'S CONTROL PROGRAM
  1 S        2 #
             3 N      28 A
             4 S       6 N
                       7 S       9 N
                                10 S      12 N      25 A
                       15 S      17 N     26 A
            20 S       22 N      27 A
            24 #

            #A N N A A A#
```

Figure 21. Surface tree for alternative program

Example 3—Control by indices

Zwicky (1966) considers the following method of control of cycling:

a.   Instances of S in a base tree are indexed as follows:
(1) Any instance of S that does not dominate an S receives the index 1.
(2) Any instance of S that dominates other instances of S receives the index $N + 1$ if (a) every dominated S is indexed, and (b) the maximum index of a dominated S is N.

b.   On the Nth pass through the rules, transformations are applied to all subtrees dominated by an S with index N and to no other subtrees.

This algorithm is, like the two already discussed, a bottom-to-top cycle. However, it relies on predetermined indices to define the currently lowest sentence, instead of using deletion of sentence boundaries. This control program can be expressed only with difficulty in the control language, because there is no convenient way of marking indices. The following program is an inelegant but accurate expression of Zwicky's scheme—it uses inherent features INDEX1, ..., INDEXN to mark indices. The maximum possible depth of a tree must be known beforehand; the program below works only up to depth 4.

Four transformations are used to insert indices; four more are used in IN-constructs. Transformations INDEX1, ..., INDEX4 insert feature specifications which correspond to the indices above:

```
TRANS INDEX1 .
SD 1S , WHERE 1 NDOM S .
SC | + INDEX1 | MERGEF 1 .

TRANS INDEX2 .
SD 1S/⟨ % S | + INDEX1 | % ⟩ .
SC | + INDEX2 | MERGEF 1 .

TRANS INDEX3.
SD 1S/⟨ % S | + INDEX2 | % ⟩ .
SC | + INDEX3 | MERGEF 1 , | + INDEX2 | ERASEF 1 .

TRANS INDEX4 .
SD 1S/⟨ % S | + INDEX3 | % ⟩.
SC | + INDEX4 | MERGEF 1 , | + INDEX3 + INDEX2 | ERASEF 1 .
```

Transformations FIRST, SECOND, THIRD, and FOURTH associate the integer 1 with the appropriately indexed S's.

```
TRANS FIRST .
SD 1 S | + INDEX1 | .
SC | + INDEX1 | ERASEF 1.

TRANS SECOND .
SD 1 S | + INDEX2 | .
SC | + INDEX2 | ERASEF 1.
```

TRANS THIRD .
SD 1 S |+ INDEX3 | .
SC |+ INDEX3 | ERASEF 1 .

TRANS FOURTH .
SD 1 S |+ INDEX 4 | .
SC |+ INDEX4 | ERASEF 1 .

If II is the group number for the embedding transformations, the control program can be expressed as:

INDEX1; INDEX2; INDEX3; INDEX4;
IN FIRST (1) DO ⟨ II ⟩ ;
IN SECOND (1) DO ⟨ II ⟩ ;
IN THIRD (1) DO ⟨ II ⟩ ;
IN FOURTH (1) DO ⟨ II ⟩ .

Note that the indices are erased when used; this prevents them from interfering with other tests on features.

If this program is applied to Zwicky's example:

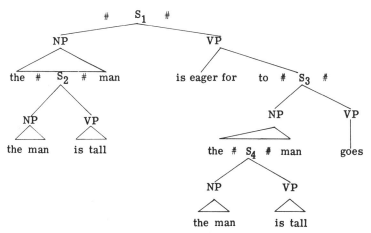

the effect is as follows:

INDEX1 merges the feature specification + INDEX1 into the complex symbols associated with S_2 and S_4.

INDEX2 merges the feature specification + INDEX2 into the complex symbols for S_1 and S_3.

INDEX3 succeeds for S_1 only. It merges the feature specification + INDEX3 into the complex symbol and erases the feature + INDEX2.

INDEX4 fails.

After these first four transformations the tree is (schematically):

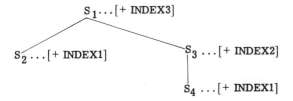

The remaining instructions invoke the embedding transformations for S_2, S_4, S_3, and S_1, as desired, and delete all occurrences of the index features.

An alternative representation of this algorithm is given on p. 121.

ORDER OF INSTRUCTIONS

In the examples already given, it is sufficient to do the instructions in the order given without any branching in the program. However, one would like to be able to choose the next instruction on the basis of what has happened so far. This facility is provided by IF-instructions, GOTO-instructions, and labels.

GOTO-instructions and labels

9. 01   *control-program* ::= sclist[opt[*label* :] *instruction*]

9. 02   *label* ::= *word*

9. 12   *GOTO-instruction* ::= GOTO *label*

The simplest change in the linear flow of control is provided by allowing transfer to a labeled instruction. Any instruction in a control program can be labeled by preceding it with a *word* and a colon. Control can be transferred to a labeled instruction, say DO1, by a *GOTO-instruction* GOTO DO1. Thus, the control program

CP FIRST: TRAN1; TRAN2; GOTO FIRST; TRAN3.

invokes transformations in the order TRAN1, TRAN2, TRAN1, TRAN2, TRAN1, ... This program contains an infinite loop, but *GOTO-instructions* can be combined with *IF-instructions* to create reasonable programs.

Conditional instructions

The form of a conditional instruction or *IF-instruction* is given by:

9. 08   *IF-instruction* ::= IF-*instruction* THEN *GOTO-instruction*
                  opt[ELSE *GOTO-instruction*] []
                  IF *FLAG-name* THEN *GOTO-instruction* opt[
                  ELSE *GOTO-instruction*]

For example,

IF TRAN1 THEN GOTO EMB

or

IF TRAN2 THEN GOTO EMB ELSE GOTO CONJ

where EMB and CONJ are labels and TRAN1 and TRAN2 are transformation names.

The *instruction* between IF and THEN may be of any type. For each type of instruction there is a rule for computing an associated value. The simplest case is an instruction which is a transformation name: the value is true if the transformation has been invoked, the structural description has been matched, and the structural change, if any, has been carried out; the value is false otherwise.

Value determination and *FLAG-name* are discussed in separate sections below. The interpretation of an IF-instruction is that first the *instruction* between IF and THEN is performed. If the resulting value is true the GOTO-instruction after THEN is performed, otherwise the GOTO-instruction after ELSE is performed. If the ELSE-clause is omitted and the value is false the next instruction is performed.

In using an IF-instruction it is important to note that in

IF T1 THEN GOTO A; T2; A:T3

T1 is invoked for all S's in the tree, and if it is successful for at least one then T2 is bypassed for all S's. Most often, a grammar requires not this pattern, but conditional application with a given S. Placing the IF-instruction within an IN-instruction can restrict condition and consequence to a single S:

IN NEXTS(1) DO ⟨ IF T1 THEN GOTO A; T2; A:T3 ⟩

If the structural description for NEXTS is % 1 S %, the S's are considered one at a time, and the invocation of T2 in a particular S is conditional on the previous failure of T1 in that S.

Example 4—A use of conditional instructions

Klevansky's "A Transformational Grammar for Swahili" (1968) makes use of conditional instructions. Basically, each transformation is called by its transformation name. However, the transformations QNANI, QNINI and QLINI are optional and are alternatives; conditional instructions ensure that the structural change for at most one of them is carried out.

```
CP  INSERTKU; PREAGV; NEGSUB;
    REL1; REL2; ANPRE1; ANPRE2;
    IF QNANI THEN GOTO E;
    IF QNINI THEN GOTO E;
    IF QLINI THEN GOTO E;
E:  STOP .
```

FLAG-INSTRUCTIONS

An *IF-instruction* that begins

IF *instruction* THEN ...

performs the instruction, tests its value, and then discards the value. Flags and FLAG-instructions provide a means for deferred testing of values. Flags store values so that IF-instructions can test them later. An IF-instruction that begins

IF *FLAG-name* THEN ...

tests information about whether certain transformations and groups of transformations have previously applied and uses that history to change the present course of the program.

9.09   *FLAG-instruction* ::= *FLAG-name transformation-list*

9.10   *FLAG-name* ::= **FLAG** opt[*integer*]

9.11   *transformation-list* ::= *transformation-element* []
        ⟨ sclist[*transformation-element*] ⟩

Flags take on the values true and false. They are distinguished from one another by *integer*s: FLAG 1, FLAG 2, ... A *FLAG-name* without an *integer* refers to FLAG 0. (The implementation of the control language provides ten flags numbered from zero to nine.)

The *FLAG-instruction*

FLAG 3 ⟨ II; TRAN4 ⟩

illustrates all of the formats. It associates FLAG 3 with the transformations of group II and TRAN4. The *IF-instruction*

IF FLAG 3 THEN GOTO A

transfers control to A if any one of these transformations applies successfully between execution of the FLAG-instruction and the IF-instruction.

More generally, a FLAG-instruction means:

1. Discard any previous value or definition the flag may have.

2. Define the flag to represent the transformations and groups in the transformation list.

3. Set the value of the flag to false.

The value of a flag remains false until one of the transformations that it represents is invoked and has value true (that is, its structural description is matched and its structural change, if any, is applied); it thereupon becomes true. The value remains true until the flag is redefined by a FLAG-instruction.

For example, a flag representing transformations T1, T2, and T3 is defined by the FLAG-instruction:

FLAG 5 ⟨ T1; T2; T3 ⟩

Flag 5 is set to false when this instruction is executed. Thereafter, if any of its three transformations is invoked and has value true, flag 5 is set to true. Flag 5 retains the value true until it is redefined. (If flag 5 is redefined as T1, T2, T3, then its value is just reset to false.)

The next two programs illustrate resetting a flag. In the first, flag 1 is reset for each subtree. In the second it is not reset, so if T5 applies to any subtree, T6 is never invoked again.

CP IN LOWESTS(1) DO ⟨ FLAG 1 T5; II; IF FLAG 1 THEN GOTO END;
    T6; END : T7 ⟩.
CP FLAG 1 T5; IN LOWESTS(1) DO ⟨ II; IF FLAG 1 THEN GOTO END;
    T6; END : T7 ⟩.

RPT-INSTRUCTIONS

To invoke repetitively a transformation, a group of transformations, or a control program, a RPT-instruction may be used.

9.07   *RPT-instruction* ::= RPT opt[*integer*]⟨ *control-program* ⟩

If the optional *integer* is omitted, the subprogram is repeated until all of its instructions have the value false. The *integer* imposes a maximum on the number of executions of the subprogram. For example,

CP RPT 5 ⟨ TRAN1; TRAN2; III ⟩

repeats the sequence

invoke TRAN1

invoke TRAN2

invoke group III

until either no transformation applies or five iterations of the sequence have occurred.

An example of a RPT-instruction without an integer is

RPT ⟨ II; TRAN3 ⟩

This instruction invokes every transformation in group II and then transformation TRAN3 and repeats this process until none of the transformations in group II applies and TRAN3 does not apply. Then the RPT-instruction terminates. Note that it is possible to create infinite loops with RPT-instructions.

A *RPT-instruction* may include any *control-program*, and in particular may include other *RPT-instruction*s. So,

    RPT 4 ⟨ III; RPT ⟨ IV ⟩ ; TRAN4 ⟩

invokes the transformations of group III, then invokes group IV repetitively until none of its transformations applies, then invokes transformation TRAN4; this whole sequence is performed at most four times.

Example 5 — A use of RPT

The RPT-instruction can be used to give the bottom-to-top cycle of Example 3 an almost equivalent representation that works for arbitrarily deep trees.[2] Again, feature specifications are used as indices. Initially each S is marked (by MARK) to indicate that it has not yet been used as top node; it loses this specification when it is selected (by FIRST) as top node. The repeated sub-program first identifies all the currently lowest sentences (by LOWS), then uses them one at a time as top node. The important point is that all the lowest sentences are identified at the beginning of the block, so that sentences that become lowest by application of a transformation in the subprogram are not selected until the next cycle.

```
"EXAMPLE 5"
TRANSFORMATIONS
TRANS MARK.
        SD 1 S.
        SC | +I2 | MERGEF 1.
TRANS LOWS.
        SD 1 S | +I2 | ¬/⟨ % S | +I2 | % ⟩.
        SC | + I1 | MERGEF 1.
TRANS FIRST.
        SD 1 S | + I1 |.
        SC | +I1 +I2 | ERASEF 1.
"INSERT HERE TRANSFORMATIONS OF GROUP II"
CP MARK; RPT ⟨ LOWS; IN FIRST(1) DO ⟨ II ⟩⟩.
                $END
```

Transformation of the tree represented schematically as:

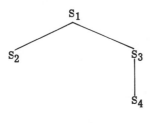

---

2 It is possible to invent grammars for which these programs are not equivalent by using the structural changes to create new nodes S. In such cases both programs would very likely be unsatisfactory.

is accomplished by this program in the following steps:

MARK

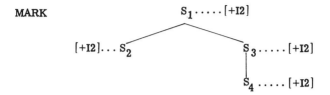

LOWS

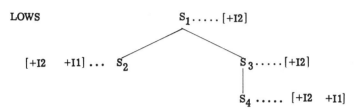

IN FIRST(1) DO < II >

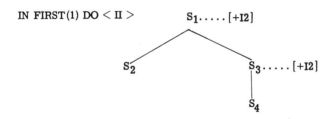

LOWS

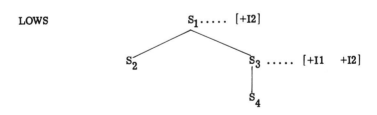

IN FIRST(1) DO < II >

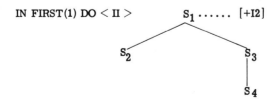

LOWS

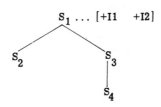

IN FIRST(1) DO ⟨ II ⟩

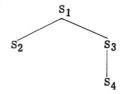

THE VALUE OF AN INSTRUCTION

Each instruction of the control language has a value: true or false. A value true means that some change has been made to the tree (or that a transformation without structural change has applied).

The simplest instruction is the name of a transformation. Such an instruction has value true only if the structural description of the transformation is met at least once in the current tree. If the transformation has a structural change, then a true value also implies that this change has been made at least once. If the structural description does not match, or if, because of optionality, the structural change is not applied, the value is false.

Group numbers denote sets of transformations. The value of a group number is true if at least one of the transformations in its set has value true and is false otherwise.

*Transformation-name*s and *group-number*s may be grouped together into a *transformation-list* by enclosing them in angular brackets. The value of a transformation list is true if any transformation or group number within the list is true and is false otherwise.

GO-instructions, TRACE-instructions and STOP-instructions have no values. Within the computer implementation of the control language these instructions are given the value false.

A RPT-instruction takes the value of the control program contained in it: if any instruction within the RPT-instruction is true, then the value of the RPT-instruction is true; it is false otherwise.

An IN-instruction takes the value true if the transformation named after the IN is true and is false otherwise. Note that this is equivalent to saying that an IN-instruction takes the value true if the list of instructions following the DO is executed at least once.

A FLAG-name has no value unless it is used within an *IF-instruction*. Then its value is the value of the flag that it denotes.

Finally, the value of a *control-program* is true if any instruction within the *control-program* has value true and is false otherwise.

STOP-INSTRUCTION

The STOP-instruction terminates the execution of a control program; it may appear at any point.

9. 15   *STOP-instruction* ::= STOP

In the implementation a STOP-instruction outputs the final tree and lists the transformations that have applied in the order in which they were invoked.

A control program need not contain a STOP-instruction. The end of the control program acts as a STOP-instruction.

TRACING THE APPLICATION OF TRANSFORMATIONS

So far we have described only instructions that contribute to the linguistic content of the transformational component. The control language also contains instructions to follow the application of transformations and output the tree when certain conditions arise.

The simplest such instruction is TREE, which causes the tree to be printed out. For example, if the control program of Example 1 is changed to

CP IN LOWESTS(1) DO ⟨ I; TREE ⟩ ; II.

the tree is output each time group I has been invoked for a lowest sentence. The result for this extended example is that trees (8), (9), and (10) are output. Tree (11), the final result, is automatically output without special instructions. If only the final result (10) of the cyclic transformations is wanted, the program becomes:

CP IN LOWESTS(1) DO ⟨ I ⟩ ; TREE; II.

To provide more selective output, the language contains instructions that enable the linguist to trace transformations and groups of transformations:

9. 13   *TRACE-instruction* ::= TRACE *transformation-list   trace-specification* [] UNTRACE *transformation-list* [] TREE

9. 14   *trace-specification* ::= BEFORE TEST [] AFTER SUCCESS [] AFTER FAILURE [] AFTER CHANGE

A trace begins when TRACE is encountered and terminates at a corresponding UNTRACE. If a transformation that is being traced is invoked, the tree is output whenever the specified point in the process is reached. BEFORE TEST means after all keywords are satisfied, but before analysis. AFTER FAILURE means after analysis has tried but failed to match the structural description. AFTER SUCCESS means after the structural description is matched. AFTER CHANGE means after the structural change is made.

For example,

TRACE TRAN5 AFTER SUCCESS

causes the tree to be output each time the analysis procedure reports success in matching the structural description of TRAN5. The output occurs just before the corresponding structural change is made.

Any number of transformations may be traced at one time, and any combination of specifications may apply to a given transformation at one time. For example,

TRACE ⟨ TRAN6; I ⟩ BEFORE TEST;
TRACE I AFTER CHANGE

outputs the tree just before analysis for TRAN6 or any transformation in group I. In addition, each time a transformation in group I applies, the tree is output just after the structural change is made.

CHAPTER 10

The Computer Program and Its Use

The first nine chapters emphasize the nature of the model and say little about the computer implementation. For several reasons, a discussion of the program is also important. First, the program was invaluable in the development of the model. A computer program is, after all, a precise specification of an algorithm. Ideas were worked out in constructing the program and were tested by running it. Decisions sometimes had unexpected consequences and a number of changes to the model came about because of difficulties made apparent by computer runs. Our confidence in the model is based in part on the fact that the program exists and works correctly for the examples which have been tested.

Secondly, the program was designed to be used by linguists in writing grammars. A discussion of the program gives the reader an opportunity to estimate its potential usefulness to him. And finally, certain ideas in the program may be suggestive to others who are designing programs for use in linguistics.

LANGUAGE AND MACHINE

Fortran IV was selected as the programming language, even though it is generally unsuited to string manipulation. This decision was made because Fortran is maintained at many locations, where other languages may be unavailable or not maintained. Since we did not wish the use of the program to be limited to the installation where it was developed, this widespread availability of Fortran outweighed its shortcomings.

To avoid the problems with string-handling that are inherent in Fortran, an input/output subroutine package (Doran, 1967) was written to handle free-field data. As a result, the program does not have the usual limitation to fixed-field input. All formats are free-field, and input words may be up to 40 characters long.

Fortran compilers vary in the amount of freedom allowed in using certain constructions. Of particular importance for this program is the fact that only the Fortran H compiler allows character manipulation using LOGICAL* 1 variables. The program was originally written using the H compiler and this facility for character manipulation was widely used. Later, in order to obtain a version for the Fortran G compiler, we had to rewrite most of the character-handling code. The resulting version is more awkward, but can be used at more installations.

The program consists of approximately 10, 000 lines of Fortran code (including comments). The object code, with storage areas, occupies approximately 300, 000 bytes of core. The program has run on the IBM 360/67 at Stanford

University under the IBM OS operating system, and on the 360/67 at The University of Michigan under the Michigan terminal system, MTS. Although at Michigan the program can be run on-line, the program was not designed to be interactive, so no advantage is gained. The program is fully documented in a "Programmers' Manual" (Friedman *et al.*, 1968).

STRUCTURE

The program is built up of subroutines, many of which are entered from more than one point in the program. The basic idea of the program structure can be seen from Figure 22, which is a highly simplified schematic of the interrelationships of the subroutines. Arrows point from calling routine to called subroutine. In Table 2 a very brief description is given for each of the subroutines shown in Figure 22. These descriptions are incomplete and are intended only to identify the subroutines so that the figure can be interpreted.

From the figure it can be seen that MAIN is the controlling program. MAIN consists almost entirely of subroutine calls. A run begins with a call to the input routine for grammars (GRAMIN). GRAMIN in turn calls subroutines to initialize the program (INIT), and to read the parts of a grammar—phrase structure (PSGINN), lexicon (LEXIN), and transformations (TRANIN). Control then returns to MAIN and either TRIN or FTRIN is called for tree input. The tree may be a base tree with or without lexical items, or may be a skeleton. If a skeleton was read, the generation routine (GEN) is now called, and it in turn calls the lexical insertion routine (LEXINS). If a base tree was read in, lexical insertion is optional. After the base tree is complete, the user's control program for transformations is interpreted (by CONTRL) to apply the transformations. Finally the surface tree is printed out. The process then repeats either from the same base or skeleton or with new inputs.

The user has some freedom to specify which subroutines are called by MAIN; the user's input to the MAIN program is discussed below.

USE OF THE PROGRAM

Typically, the user begins with a small grammar and gradually adds to it. As lexical items or transformations are added they are tested in the context of all previous rules and their effects are examined.

The easiest errors to detect and repair in a grammar are syntactic errors. As a grammar is read in by the program a check is made for formal correctness. For each error a comment is produced which attempts to explain what is wrong. The program then continues to read in the rest of the grammar, recovering as best it can from the error. In most cases a single error causes a small part of the grammar to be read badly, but the rest of the grammar is read in and used in whatever tests are requested. We attempted to make the error comments as clear and explicit as possible, and to make the program continue despite input errors.

Deeper errors arise when a grammar is syntactically correct, but does not correctly describe the language of which it purports to be a grammar. These errors cannot be detected directly by the program, since it has no standard of

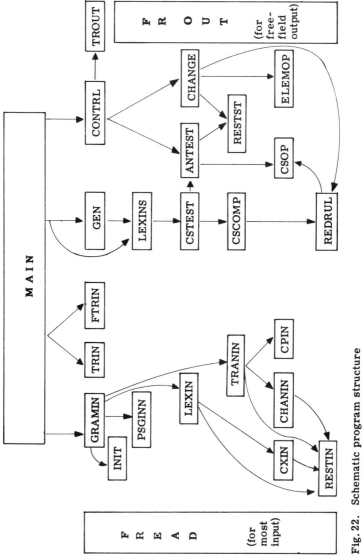

Fig. 22.   Schematic program structure

TABLE 2

Subroutine Structure

Note: The actual structure of the program has been greatly simplified by the omission of subroutines called from one routine only. Also omitted are output programs, which exist for almost every part of a grammar.

2.1   Main program

Routine	*Role*
MAIN	Reads the user's directions for the current run, and carries them out.

2.2   Free-field input/output

Routine	*Role*
FREAD	Free-field read. Returns a word or special character for each call.
FROUT	Free-field write. Outputs a designated area of storage.

2.3   Trees

Routine	*Role*
TRIN	Inputs a tabular tree.
TROUT	Outputs a tabular tree.
FTRIN	Inputs a linear tree specification.

2.4   Grammar input

Routine	*Role*
INIT	Initializes everything.
GRAMIN	Reads in a transformational grammar.
PSGINN	Inputs phrase structure rules, expands and stores them.
LEXIN	Reads in a lexicon.
TRANIN	Reads in the transformations.
CPIN	Reads in the control program.
CHANIN	Reads in a structural change.
CXIN	Reads in a structural description, contextual feature, or complex symbol.
RESTIN	Reads in a restriction.

2.5   Phrase structure generation

Routine	*Role*
GEN	Generates a directed random tree.

2.6   Lexical insertion

Routine	*Role*
LEXINS	Does lexical insertion.
CSTEST	Finds a compatible complex symbol for lexical insertion, and does side-effects for contextual features.
CSCOMP	Tests complex symbols for compatibility.

TABLE 2 (continued)

2.7   Analysis

Routine	*Role*
ANTEST	Evaluates a structural description against a subtree.

2.8   Restrictions

Routine	*Role*
RESTST	Tests a restriction.

2.9   Structural change

Routine	*Role*
CHANGE	Performs the structural change.
ELEMOP	Does tree operations.

2.10   Complex symbol operations

Routine	*Role*
REDRUL	Applies the redundancy rules to expand a complex symbol.
CSOP	Tests complex symbols and performs complex symbol operations.

2.11   Control program

Routine	*Role*
CONTRL	Interprets the control program.

---

comparison. The program tries to provide enough information to the linguist so that he will be able to see and investigate the problem.

The information produced by the program consists of derivations that may be partially controlled by the user. Since random derivations are of relatively little interest, the system allows the user to control the sentences to be generated so that they are relevant to his current problem. It is only in the sense of providing feedback to the user that the system can be called a "grammar tester"; it does not directly seek out errors in a grammar, nor does it evaluate the grammar.

Program inputs

For a standard run of the system the inputs are a grammar, a $MAIN card, and some trees. The grammar consists of one or more of *phrase-structure, lexicon,* and *transformations.* The $MAIN card is a specification of the type of run to be made. The system must be told (1) what type of input trees to expect:

TRIN, for tabular tree

FTRIN, for linear tree specification

(2) whether to generate a tree around a skeletal input or whether it is necessary only to insert lexical items:

GEN, to generate a tree and insert lexical items

LEX, to insert lexical items

and (3) whether or not to apply transformations:

TRAN, if transformations are to be applied.

The general form of the $MAIN card can be represented as

$$\$MAIN \left\{ {TRIN \atop FTRIN} \right\} \left((n) \left\{ {GEN \atop LEX} \right\} \right) (TRAN) .$$

The integer n specifies the number of times each input tree is to be used. The $MAIN card must end with a period.

As an example,

$MAIN   TRIN   GEN   TRAN .

specifies a run in which a skeletal tree is read in tabular form, a full tree is generated, including lexical items, and the transformations are applied.

The specification

$MAIN   TRIN   5   LEX   TRAN .

might be used in testing a lexicon and transformations against a fixed base tree. The tree is read and five cases of lexical insertion plus transformation are carried out.

$MAIN   FTRIN   4   LEX .

computes four examples of lexical insertion for each of the linear trees input.

After the process is completed for one input, another input is read and the cycle repeats. A run terminates when there are no more inputs.

Program output

The output of the program traces the history of the derivation step by step. Certain key subroutines in the program, such as LEXINS, ANTEST, and CONTRL write messages every time they are entered. This enables the course of lexical insertion and transformation to be traced in detail. The lexical insertion routine outputs the number of the node currently under consideration so that the order of insertion can be seen. The message written by analysis program includes the name of the transformation, and the top of the tree for the analysis.

The tree itself is output initially, after generation, after lexical insertion, and after transformation. In addition, the TREE and TRACE instructions in the control program for the transformations cause the tree to be output under specified conditions.

A uniform convention for error messages is used throughout the program. The standard form is

ERROR. Subroutine name. Message.

For example,

ERROR. TRIN. ROOT NOT SENTENCE SYMBOL. P
ERROR. CXIN. , FOLLOWED BY) IN ANALYSIS
ERROR. ANTEST. TOO MANY POSSIBLE ANALYSES. ($> = 10$)
ERROR. LEXINS. THERE ARE NO LEXICAL ITEMS SUITABLE FOR
INSERTION AT NODE 31

Lines of the form

WARNING. Subroutine name. Message.

are issued when a strong possibility of error exists. For example,

WARNING. NUMNAM. FEATURE ADSTRACT ADDED AS INHERENT

The output is written on several different logical output units, which need not all be printed. Thus, outputs designed primarily for use in system debugging need not be seen by system users.

EARLY EXPERIMENTS

The system has been in use since February 1968, although not fully complete at that time. The first experiments were carried out by the designers of the system, using grammars based on material in the linguistic literature. This was done to provide test material for the program, but, more importantly, to help ensure that the notational conventions would be adequate. A fragment of grammar from Chomsky's *Aspects* was used to test ideas and programs for lexical insertion. The Core grammar of Rosenbaum and Lochak (1966) was used in developing and testing the transformational component.

Aspects and Core provided separate examples of lexicon and transformations. There was at first no single source which contained both. A relatively formal grammar was needed, even though a final translation into the notation of the system would still of course be necessary. Elizabeth Closs Traugott's *Deep and Surface Structure in Alfredian Prose* (1967) appeared at about that time and was the first grammar which was formalized in the notation after the fact. Considerable effort had gone into designing the notation; we were anxious to see if it would now seem natural for a grammar which was entirely new. "Alfred" was thus the first real test for the system. It was considered a success because in spite of a few difficulties, the results of the run were revealing about the grammar.

Also during the spring of 1969, two sets of runs were made with preliminary versions of a grammar being developed by the U.C.L.A. Air Force English Syntax Project. This grammar was not based entirely on the *Aspects* model, but incorporated some recent ideas on case in English.

The program was also used in its early stages by L. Klevansky, who wrote a grammar of Swahili for the dual purposes of testing the programs and learning the language.

One general effect, which was noticed in the first few experiments, has continued to be striking: a major advantage of using the system is that the notation provides a framework in which grammars must be stated precisely; this need for precision forces the consideration of interesting problems which might not otherwise be noticed.

These early experiments are collected in "Computer Experiments in Transformational Grammar." (Friedman, 1968) This report gives the grammars as well as discussions of the results of the computer runs.

OBSERVATIONS ON THE EXPERIMENTS

In this section we give some examples of problems that were found by computer runs of the grammars just mentioned. The examples illustrate the types of problems that may be expected in initial computer runs of any grammar.

Trivial errors

The most common initial problems are errors in transcription of a grammar. Some of these are caused by learning a new notation; others are simply typographical. These errors are of no linguistic interest; having to deal with them is one of the prices of using the computer. In general, they can be caught with relative ease.

More than one grammar has had simple errors with respect to repetition of a transformation. Number agreement transformations are written so that they produce CAT S S S ... where CAT S is wanted. (The grammar as written calls for an infinite sequence of S's to be added. The program, more cautious, adds ten S's, then complains and goes on to the next transformation.)

Transformations are often stated so that they fail to apply in some cases where it is intended they apply. For example, the structural description of PASSIVE as

    SD # (PRE) 3NP AUX 5V (PREP) 7NP % 10P % # ,
        WHERE ¬ 3 EQ 7 .

fails to take into account some additional parts of the VP.

Correction to

    SD # (PRE) 3NP AUX (HAVE EN) (BE ING) 5V (PREP) 7NP
        % PREP 10P % # , WHERE ¬ 3 EQ 7.

allows PASSIVE to work in the additional cases. Similarly, a NOMINAL-AGREEMENT transformation which marks subjects as +NOMIN must apply not only to pronouns which precede verbs but also to those which precede copulas. Thus the structural description

    SD # % 3 (PRON , REL) V % # .

must be replaced by

SD # % 3 (PRON , REL) (V , COP) % # .

Interrelatedness of transformations

A slightly more interesting set of problems found in the computer runs are those which arise through the interrelatedness of two or more transformations. For example, in one of the grammars there were both WH-questions and TAG-questions. The TAG transformation was (optionally) applicable to any question, so that for example

TOM HAS PREFER EN WHAT GIRL HAS TOM NOT

was produced. This error was easily repaired once it was detected.

On the other hand, a similar problem which was not easily fixed arose with another transformation which was marked optional. Testing showed that for certain base trees the result was bad if the transformation did not apply; however, when the transformation was temporarily changed to obligatory, the grammar then failed to produce some intended sentences. The proper correction to the grammar would require specification of the contexts in which the transformation was obligatory.

Deep structure problems

Two of the grammars which have been studied suffer problems with the WH-morpheme when it occurs in nonsentences and not as a relative marker. Thus, for example, the generated sentences

WHAT BLAME MAY NT BE BE ING

and

WHICH THING MUST HAVE BE EN APPROVE ING OF WHAT TABLE

are in fact even worse than they appear, because they are not questions. Although this problem is linguistic rather than computational, the inputs to the program can be controlled to avoid generating sentences of this form.

Surface structure

The surface structure associated with a sentence derivation is much easier to study if it can be produced automatically. In several cases it has been apparent from the information provided by the computer runs that revisions in the grammar were needed if the surface structure was to be at all reasonable. This is a case where the computer runs are certainly not necessary, but where they reduce the tediousness of studying the problem.

INSTRUCTIONAL USE

The system has been used by Szilard Szabo in teaching *general linguistics* at the University of San Francisco, by Michael O'Malley in a course in *natural language structure* at the University of Michigan, and by Joyce Friedman in courses in *computational linguistics* at Stanford and Michigan.

The method of use is to make available a file of one or more grammars to be used as examples and as bases for modifications. The students are then asked to make modifications and additions to the grammars. The "Fragments from *Aspects*" and the Core grammar have been most useful, although small grammars written for the purpose have also been used.

For graduate students, a reasonable exercise for a term paper is to read a current journal article on transformational grammar, and then show how the results can be incorporated into the basic grammar, or show why they cannot be. The papers chosen by the students have generally been ones in which transformations are actually given. This project has been very successful as an introduction to transformational grammar for computer science students.

Other students have chosen simply to use the computer to obtain fully developed examples of derivations illustrating aspects of grammar in which they are interested.

These experiences have confirmed our belief that specific examples presented by the computer, and the feedback provided when a grammar is modified, are invaluable in clarifying the notion of transformational grammar.

LINGUISTIC RESEARCH

As of July, 1969 the system has been used for substantial work in three natural languages: French, Japanese, and Serrano.

The research in French began with the grammar of Querido (1969). This grammar is based on the form of the Core grammar; it was therefore easily translated into the notation of the computer model. Shortly after the grammar was received a large part of it was running on the computer. Minor errors were found and corrected. However, in contrast with the early experiments, the work in French was not stopped once an adequate transcription into the system had been achieved. Instead of trying to remain faithful to the original grammar, the analysis was carried further, making changes whenever the output of the program seemed to contradict linguistic data. The resulting grammar reorders the transformations, extends the analysis to several new constructions, and makes an interesting use of Chomsky-adjunction and complex symbols on higher nodes (see Morin, 1969).

Research in Japanese syntax, with particular reference to the verb system, is being carried out by Susumu Nagara and Donald Smith. Preliminary results are described in Nagara and Smith (1970).

Kenneth Hill has transcribed his grammar of Serrano, an American Indian language, (Hill, 1967) into the format of the system, and is using the computer for further research.

CONCLUSIONS

Interesting changes to the model have been suggested by actual experience in using the system. Difficulties in the Core grammar suggested the repetition AAC. Chomsky-adjunction was added after the model was complete in order to satisfy a user. We intend to add methods of representing and handling constraints on variables, and other notions such as command and islands (Ross, 1967), as users begin to rely on these concepts in constructing grammars. The interaction between model-building and grammar-writing will thus continue. The authors are gratified by the enthusiasm of linguists using the system, but are aware that constant change and increased flexibility are required to maintain it as a useful tool for linguistic research.

An Example of Grammar and Derivation

```
            "MONTREAL FRENCH"
        PHRASESTRUCTURE
        S      = # (PRE) SN SV (PASSIF) # .
        PRE    = (INT) (NEG) .
        SV     = V (SN) (SN) .
        SN     = ((SN) S, (DET) N) .
        DET    = ((DEF,QUEL))(CARD) .
        DEF    = (CET ((CI,LA)),LE) .
            $ENDPSG
        LEXICON
         CATEGORY N  V CARD .
         INHERENT PLUR FEM EE PERS TWOPERS HUM ANIM ABST
                  NOMIN ACCUS
                  EMP PPRCN PRCN REL REF TON
                  VE ADJ FUTUR PRET PRCG SUBJ INF PASSIF
                  ASN DESN SNASN SNDESN
                  ACSUBJ POP XETRE ANTACJ ELCOMP
                  DELSUJ INFPRCP TRINF CEINF ACJPR DASHY
                  PROCARD .
          CONTEXTUAL
            NCOM   = <SN<DET_>>,
            NPRO   = <SN/<LE_>>,
            ANTCON = <SN<SN<%_>S>>,
            PLURAL = <SN/<%_N|+PLUR|>>,
            IMPERS = <S/<%S_%>>,
            INTR   = <S/<%_#>>,
            PROP   = <SV/<_S>>,
            UNTR   = <SV<_SN>>,
            DEUXTR = <SV<_SN SN>>,
            PASCON = <S/<%_% PASSIF #>>,
            IDSUJ  = <S/<% 1SN SV/<_S/<% 2SN V %>> %>, WHERE 1 EQ 2>,
            IDOBJ  = <SV/<_S/<% 1SN V %> 2SN>,WHERE 1 EQ 2>.
          RULES
            |+SNASN|     => |+DELXTR|,
            |+SNDESN|    => |+DELXTR|,
            |+ASN|       => |-PASCON|,
            |+DESN|      => |-PASCON|,
            |+ADJ|       => |-PASCON|,
            |+IMPERS|    => |+ACSUBJ|.
          ENTRIES
            UN       |+CARD -PLURAL|,
            DEUX     |+CARD +PLURAL|,
            UNPEUD   |+CARD +PROCARD +PLURAL|,
            CHOSE    |+N +FEM -PLUR -HUM +PPRON|,
            DIEU     |+N +NPRO -FEM -PLUR +HUM|
            DIEU     |+N -FEM -PLUR +HUM +PPRON|,
            ENFANT   |+N +NCOM *FEM +EE *PLUR +HUM|,
            JEAN     |+N -FEM -PLUR +HUM +NPRO|,
            FILLE    |+N +NCOM +FEM +EE +PLUR|,
            LIVRE    |+N +NCCM -FEM *PLUR -HUM|,
            PERS     |+N *FEM +EE *PLUR +HUM -NCCM -ANTCON +PERS *TWOPERS|,
            PERSON   |+N +FEM +EE -PLUR +HUM +PPRCN|,
            CROIT    |+V +DASHY +ASN +ELCCMP +UNTR -IMPERS *PRET *PROG *FUTUR|,
            DEMAND   |+V +SNASN +TRINF +DEINF -IMPERS *PRET *PROG *FUTUR|,
            DIT      |+V +SNASN *DELSUJ -IMPERS *PRET *PROG *FUTUR|,
            DIT      |+V +SNASN +IDOBJ +CEINF -IMPERS *PRET *PROG *FUTUR|,
            DONNE    |+V +SNASN -IMPERS *PRET *PRCG *FUTUR|,
            LEVE     |+V *PRET *PROG *FUTUR +UNTR -IMPERS|,
            OSE      |+V +UNTR +IDSUJ -PASCCN -IMPERS *PRET *PROG *FUTUR *PROG|,
```

```
REGARD      |+V +PRET -PROG -FUTUR +UNTR -IMPERS|,
SOURIT      |+V -DEUXTR +ASN -IMPERS *PRET *FUTUR *PROG|,
VIENT       |+V +INTR -IMPERS *PRET *PROG *FUTUR +XETRE|,
VOIT        |+V +INFPROP +UNTR -IMPERS *PRET *PROG *FUTUR|,
JOLI        |+V +ADJ +INTR -PRET -PROG -FUTUR +ANTADJ|,
NECESS      |+V +ADJ -DEUXTR +ASN *PRET *PROG *FUTUR|,
.      $ENDLEX
TRANSFORMATIONS
TRANS 0 LOWESTS III (#).
SD 1 S ¬/<% S<# % #> %>, WHERE 1 DCM #.
     "TRANSFORMATIONS CYCLIQUES"
     "COMPLEMENTATION"
TRANS  10 ADJQUE "INTRODUCTION DE QUE-FINI" I AACC (S) .
   SD # % SN< (SN) 3S > % # .
   SC QUE AFIDE 3 .
TRANS  20 ADJPR "PROPOSITION ADJECTIVALE"  OP (S) .
   SD # % 2SV/< 3V|+ADJPR| 4S/< 5QUE 6SN 7V|+ADJ| %> %> % # .
   SC ERASE 5 , 6 ARISE 3 , |+INF| MERGEF 7 , 4 ACHRE 2 .
TRANS  30 INFPROP "PROPOSITION INFINITIVE" (S) .
   SD # % 2SV/<3V|+INFPROP| 4S/< 5QUE 6SN 7V %> %> % # .
   SC ERASE 5 , 6 ARISE 3 , |+INF| MERGEF 7 , 4 ACHRE 2 .
TRANS  40 DELSUJ "INFINITF INTRODUIT PAR LE SUJET" (S).
   SD # % 3SN 4V S/<5QUE (NEG) 6SN 7V %> % # ,
      WHERE 3 EQ 6 & 4 NINC1 |-DELSUJ| .
   SC ERASE 5 , ERASE 6 , |+INF| MERGEF 7 .
TRANS  50 INFSUJ "PROPOSITION INFINITIVE SUJET" (QUE) .
   SD # (PRE) S/<4QUE (PRE) 5SN 6V %> V (SN) 10SN % # ,
      WHERE 5 EQ 10 .
   SC ERASE 4 ,ERASE 5 , |+INF| MERGEF 6 .
TRANS  60 TRINF "INFINITIF INTRODUIT PAR LE COMPLEMENT" (S) .
   SD # % 4V|+TRINF| 5(SN) S/<7QUE (PRE) 8SN 9V %> 11(SN) % # ,
      WHERE 5 EQ 8 | 8 EQ 11 .
   SC ERASE 7, ERASE 8, |+INF| MERGEF 9 .
     "REAJUSTEMENT: INTRODUCTION DES PREPOSITIONS"
TRANS  70 ASN "INTRODUCTION DE A APRES LE VERBE" .
   SD # (PRE) SN V|+ASN| 6SN % # .
   SC A ACHLE 6.
TRANS  80 SNASN "INTRODUCTION DE A APRES L'OBJET" .
   SD # (PRE) SN V|+SNASN| SN 6SN % # .
   SC A ACHLE 6 .
TRANS  90 DESN "INTRODUCTION DE DE APRES LE VERBE" .
   SD # (PRE) SN V|+DESN| 6SN % # .
   SC DE ACHLE 6 .
TRANS 100 SNDESN "INTRODUCTION DE DE APRES L'OBJET".
   SD # (PRE) SN V|+SNDESN| SN 6SN % # .
   SC DE ACHLE 6 .
     "VOIX PASSIVE"
TRANS 110 POSTSUJ "POSTPOSITION DU SUJET" AAC (PASSIF).
   SD # (PRE) (1SN/< (UN) N|+PPRON|>,2SN) 3SV 4PASSIF # .
   SC ERASE 1 , 2 ALADE 3 , PAR ACHLE 2 .
TRANS 120 COPOBJ "COPIE DE L'OBJET" (PASSIF) .
   SD # (PRE) 1SV<V 2SN %> % # .
   SC 2 ADLES 1 .
TRANS 130 PASREFL "PASSIF REFLEXIF" OP (PASSIF) .
   SD # (PRE) SN<% N|-ANIM|> % 1(PAR) % 2PASSIF # .
   SC IF<NUL 1> THEN <ERASE 2> .
TRANS 140 PASPER "PASSIF PERIPHRASTIC" (PASSIF) .
   SD # % 1V 2SN % 3PASSIF # .
   SC |+PASSIF| MERGEF 1 , E ALADE 1 , ERASE 2 , ERASE 3 .
     "ACCORD VERBAL"
```

```
TRANS 150 ACPRED "ACCORD DU PRECICAT" .
SD # (PRE) SN/<% 4(N) %> 7V % .
SC |*FEM *PERS *TWOPERS *PLUR| MCVEF 4 7 , |+VE| MERGEF 7 .
   "PRONOMINALISATION"
TRANS 160 REFLEXIF .
SD # % 3N (S) V % SN/<9(DET) 1ON (S)> % # ,
   WHERE 3 EQ 10 .
SC PRON SUBSE 9 , |+REF| MERGEF 10 .
TRANS 170 PRONCM " PRONOMINALISATICN" ACAC (S) .
SD # % 3N % S/<% SN/< 7DET 8N (S)> %> % 11(N) % # ,
   WHERE 3 EQ 8 | 8 EC 11 .
SC PRON SUBSE 7 .
TRANS 180 ELLIPSE .
SD  1 # % 3 # .
SC  ERASE 1, ERASE 3.
   "TRANSFORMATICNS PCST CYCLIQUES"
   "INTRODUCTION DES PRONCMS RELATIFS"
TRANS 190 RELATIF II AACC (S) .
SD % SN/<% 4N S/<% SN/<(PRCN) 7N > %>> % ,
   WHERE 4 EC 7 .
SC |+REL| MERGEF 7,|+EMP| MERGEF 4.
TRANS 210 ACPRON "ACCORD DU PRONCM" AACC .
SD % SN/< 3(PRON,DEF,QUEL) (CARD) 5N > % .
SC |*REL *REF *FEM *PLUR *HUM *EMP| MCVEF 5 3 ,
   IF<TRM 3> THEN<ERASE 5> .
TRANS 220 ACCUS "MARQUE DE L'ACCUSATIF" .
SD % V 4(PRON,QUEL,N<PERS>) % .
SC |+ACCUS| MERGEF 4 .
TRANS 230 NOMINA "MARQUE DU NCMINATIF" .
SD % 1SN/<2(N<PERS>,PRON) (S)> SV % .
SC |+NCMIN| MERGEF 2 ,
   IF <2 INC1 |+EMP|> THEN <2 ADLAC 1 , |+TON| MERGEF 2> .
   "ACCORD NOMINAL"
TRANS 240 ELLIDET "ELLISICN CU CETERMINANT" II AACC (DET) .
SD % 1DET 2N|+NPRO -PLUR| %, WHERE 2 NINC1 |+EMP| .
SC ERASE 1 .
TRANS 250 ELLISING "ELLISION DU CARDINAL" AACC (CARD) .
SD % DET<2(*) 3CARD> 4N|-PLUR| % .
SC IF <NUL 2> THEN <|*FEM| MCVEF 4 3> ELSE <ERASE 3> .
TRANS 260 REDREL "REDUCTICN DES RELATIFS" AACC (PRON ) .
SD % 1S/< QUE 2(PRE) PRCN|+REL| 3SV<4V|-PRET -FUTUR| %>> % ,
   WHERE 4 INC1 |+ACJ| | 4 INC1 |+PASSIF| .
SC |*VE| ERASEF 3 , 2 ADLES 1 , 3 ADLES 1 , ERASE 1 .
TRANS 270 MDEM "PLACEMENT DU DEMCNSTRATIF" AACC (DET) .
SD % 1SN/< CET 2(CI,LA) N 3(SV) %> % .
SC 2 ALADE 1 .
TRANS 280 ELCOMP "ELLISION DU CCMPLEMENT" OP ACAC .
SD % V|+ELCCMP| % 5SN/<((A,DE))(UN) 6N|+PPRON|> %,
   WHERE 6 NINC1 |+EMP| .
SC ERASE 5 .
   "PERMUTATIONS"
TRANS 290 ATTINT "ATTACHEMENT DE L'INTERRCGATIF" (QUEL) .
SD 1(QUE) 2INT % 3SN/<% 4QUEL %> % .
SC ERASE 1 , QUEL1 ALADE 4 , 3 ALADE 2 .
TRANS 300 ATTREL "ATTACHEMENT DU RELATIF" ACAC (QUE) .
SD % S/< 4QUE % 5SN/<% 6(PRON|+REL|,N|+REL|)> %> % .
SC (QUEL<QUEL1>) ARISE 6 , 5 SUBSE 4 .
TRANS 310 ANTEPO1 "ANTEPOSITICN DES OBJETS DIRECTS" .
SD % 4V 5(REF,PRON,N<PERS>) % .
SC 5 ADLES 4 , IF <5 NINC1 |+EMP|> THEN < ERASE 5> .
```

```
TRANS 320 ANTEPO2 "ANTEPOSITICN DES PERSONNELS OBJETS INDIRECTS" (A) .
  SD % 4SV/<3(PRON) 5V (SN) 8SN/< A 9(PRCN|+REF|,N<PERS>) > %> ,
     WHERE 5 NINC1 |+DASHY| & 3 NINC1 |+REF| .
  SC 8 ADFID 4 , IF<9 NINC1 |+EMP|> THEN <ERASE 8> .
TRANS 330 ANTEPO3 " ANTEPOSITION DES PRONOMS OBJETS INDIRECTS" (A) .
  SD % SV/<3(PRON) 5V (SN) 8SN/<A 9PRON> %> ,
     WHERE 5 NINC1 |+DASHY| & 3 NINC1 |+REF| .
  SC 8 ADLES 5 , IF <9 NINC1 |+EMP|> THEN <ERASE 8> .
TRANS 340 ANTADJ "ANTEPOSITION DE L'ACJECTIF" AACC .
  SD % 1SN/< 2SN<DET 3N> SV<4V|+ADJ +ANTADJ|>> % , WHERE 4 NINC1 |+VF| .
  SC 4 ALESE 3 , 2 SUBSE 1 .
TRANS 350 EXTRAP "EXTRAPOSITICN" (S) .
  SD (PRE) 3S 4SV % .
  SC (PRON|+NOMIN|) ARISE 3 , 3 ARISE 4 .
TRANS 360 PERMCOMP " PERMUTATION DU COMPLEMENT INDIRECT" (S) .
  SD % 2V SN/< S > 4SN/< (A,DE) SN > % .
  SC 4 ARISE 2 .
     "REAJUSTEMENT"
TRANS 370 ADJCE "INTRODUCTION DE CE" AACC (QUE) .
  SD % (A,DE) 3S/< QUE % > % .
  SC CE ALESE 3 .
TRANS 380 DEINF "INTRODUCTICN CE DE" (S) .
  SD % V|+DEINF|  (SN) 4SN< S/< % V|+INF| % > > % .
  SC DE ACHLE 4 .
TRANS 390 ACSUBJ "ACCORD DU SUBJONCTIF-QUE NON-FINI" (S) .
  SD 1(NEG) % 2V|+ACSUBJ| S/<% 4V %> % ,
     WHERE 4 NINC1 |+INF| & (NNUL 1 | 2 NINC1 |+POP|) .
  SC |+SUBJ| MERGEF 4.
TRANS 400 ELLIPPRO "PRONOMINALISATICN DE QUEL" AACC (QUEL) .
  SD %  2QUEL 3N|+PPRON| % .
  SC |+HUM| MOVEF 3 2 , |+PRCN| MERGEF 2 , ERASE 3 .
     "TRANSFORMATIONS MORPHOLOGIQUES"
     "MORPHOLOGIE DU VERBE"
TRANS 600 MPASS "PASSIF" .
  SD % 3V|+VE| % , WHERE 3 INC1 |+ADJ| | 3 INC1 |+PASSIF| .
  SC |+PASSIF *ADJ| ERASEF 3 ,
     EST ACHLE 3 , |+V *FEM *PLUR| SAVEF 3 .
TRANS 610 MSUBJ "SUBJONCTIF" .
  SD % 2V|+SUBJ|< 3* %> % .
  SC |*PROG *SUBJ *PRET *FUTUR| ERASEF 2 , J ARISE 3 .
TRANS 620 IMPAR "IMPARFAIT" .
  SD % 2V|+PROG +PRET -FUTUR|<3* %> % ,
     WHERE 2 NINC1 |+INF| .
  SC |*PROG *PRET| ERASEF 2 , AIT ARISE 3 .
TRANS 630 METREPAS "PASSE CCMPOSE AVEC ETRE" .
  SD % 2((PRON|+REF|,N|+REF|)) 3V|+PRET|<4* %> % ,
     WHERE NNUL 2 | 3 INC1 |+XETRE| .
  SC |*PRET *PROG| ERASEF 3 , EST ACHLE 3 , E ARISE 4,
     |+V *FEM *PLUR| SAVEF 3 .
TRANS 640 MAVOIPAS "PASSE CCMPOSE AVEC AVCIR" .
  SD % 3V|+PRET|<5* %> % .
  SC |*PRET *PROG| ERASEF 3 , AV ACHLE 3 , |+V *ADJ| SAVEF 3 ,
     E ARISE 4 .
TRANS 650 MINF "INFINITIF" .
  SD % 2V|+INF|<3* %> % .
  SC R ARISE 3 , |*PROG *PRET *INF *FUTUR| ERASEF 2 .
TRANS 660 MFUTUR .
  SD % 2V|+FUTUR|<3* %> % .
  SC RA ARISE 3 , |*PROG *PRET *INF *FUTUR| ERASEF 2 .
TRANS 670 PLACENEG "NEGATICN" (NEG) .
```

```
SD % 2NEG   % 5SV<(SN) (SN) 9V<8* %> %> % .
SC IF <9 DOM R> THEN < PAS AFIDE 5> ELSE <PAS ARISE 8>,
   NE AFIDE 5 , ERASE 2 .
TRANS 680 ACCPPO "ACCORD DU PARTICIPE PASSE" (AV) .
SD % 3(PRON|+ACCUS|,QUEL|+ACCUS|) % V<AV % 6V<* E>> % .
SC |*FEM *PLUR| MOVEF 3 6 .
   "MORPHOLOGIE DES PRONOMS"
TRANS 690 PREVPRO "OBJET INDIRECT PREVERBAL" .
SD % (1A (2PRON|+REF|,3PRON,4N<PERS>),2PRON|+REF|) (PRON) V % .
SC ERASE 1 , SE AFIDE 2 , LUI| AFIDE 3 , |+EE| MERGEF 3 ,
   IF <4 INC1 |-TWOPERS|> THEN <ME SUBSE 5> ELSE <TE SUBSE 5> .
TRANS 700 POSTPRO "POSTVERBAL ET TONIQUE" ACAC .
SD % (V % (3PRON,4N<5PERS>),3PRON|+TON|,4N|+TON|<5PERS>) % ,
   WHERE TRM 3 | NUL 3 .
SC LUI AFIDE 3 ,
   IF <4 INC1 |-TWOPERS|> THEN <MOI SUBSE 5> ELSE <TOI SUBSE 5> .
TRANS 710 NOMACCPR "NOMINATIF ET ACCUSATIF" AACC .
SD % (3PRON,4N< 5PERS >) % , WHERE TRM 3 | NUL 3 .
SC IF <3 INC1 |+NOMIN| | 4 INC1 |+NOMIN|>
   THEN <IF <4 INC1 |-TWOPERS|> THEN <JE SUBSE 5> ELSE <TU SUBSE 5> ,
        IL AFIDE 3>
   ELSE <IF <4 INC1 |-TWOPERS|> THEN <ME SUBSE 5> ELSE <TE SUBSE 5> ,
        LE AFIDE 3> .
TRANS 715 GNPRON "GENRE ET NOMBRE DES PRONOMS" AACC .
SD % (1N|+PLUR|<(2JE,2ME,2MOI,3TU,3TE,3TOI)>,5PRON|+PLUR|<(6LUI1,SE)>,
   7PRON|+FEM|<8(LUI,IL)>,9PRON|-FEM +PLUR|<1OLUI>) % .
SC NOUS SUBSE 2, VOUS SUBSE 3 , LEUR SUBSE 6 , ELLE SUBSE 8 ,
   EUX SUBSE 10,|*PLUR| ERASEF 1 , |*PLUR| ERASEF 5 ,
   |*FEM| ERASEF 7 , |*FEM *PLUR| ERASEF 9 .
   "MORPHOLOGIE DES INTERROGATIFS"
TRANS 720 ADJESK "INTRODUCTION DE EST-CE QUE" (INT) .
SD 2S/<1INT %> , WHERE 2 NDOMBY 3 .
SC EST ALADE 1 , QU ALADE 1 .
TRANS 730 ADJSI "INTRODUCTION DE SI" (INT).
SD 1QUE 2INT % , WHERE TRM 2 . SC SI ALADE 2 , ERASE 1 .
TRANS 740 INTTON "FORMES TONIQUES DE L'INTERROGATIF" (QUEL) .
SD % (2QUEL|+PRON +HUM|,3QUEL|+PRON -HUM|) % .
SC QUI SUBSE 2 , QUOI SUBSE 3 .
TRANS 750 NOMACCIN "NOMINATIF ET ACCUSATIF" ACAC (INT) .
SD % INT/<(2QUOI,% 2QU) %> 3(SN) 4(SV) % , WHERE 4 NDOM R .
SC IF <NNUL 4> THEN <CE ALESE 2> ,
   IF <NUL 3 & NNUL 4> THEN <QUI SUBSE 2>
                       ELSE <QUE SUBSE 2> .
TRANS 760 CEAQUOI "INTRODUCTION DE CE" CP (QUOI) .
SD % INT/< 2(A,DE) QUOI> % . SC CE ALESE 2 .
TRANS 770 CEDONT "INTRODUCTION DE DONT" (CE DE QUOI) .
SD % INT/< CE 3DE 4QUOI> % . SC ERASE 4 , DONT SUBSE 3 .
   "MORPHOLOGIE DES RELATIFS"
TRANS 780 MREL "RELATIF" (QUEL) .
SD % (2PRON|+NOMIN|,2N|+NOMIN|,3PRON|+ACCUS|,3N|+ACCUS|,2PRON|+EMP|,
   2N,4PRON) 5QUEL % .
SC IF <NNUL 2> THEN <ERASE 2 , QUI SUBSE 5>,
   IF <NNUL 3> THEN <ERASE 3 , QUE SUBSE 5>,
   IF <NNUL 4> THEN <|*FEM *PLUR| MOVEF 4 5> .
TRANS 790 MDONT "INTRODUCTION DE DONT" CP (LE QUEL) .
SD % 2DE 3LE 4QUEL % . SC DONT SUBSE 2 , ERASE 3 , ERASE 4 .
TRANS 800 MQUI "INTRODUCTION DE QUI" OP (LE QUEL) .
SD 2PRON|+REL +HUM -PLUR| 3QUEL . SC ERASE 2 , QUI SUBSE 3 .
   "MORPHOLOGIE DU NOM,DES ADJECTIFS ET DES ARTICLES"
TRANS 810 MFEM "FEMININ" AACC .
```

```
SD % 1(N|+FEM|,DEF|+FEM|,V|+FEM|,PRON|+FEM|,QUEL|+FEM|,
        CARD|+FEM|) % ,  WHERE 1 NINC1 |+EE| & 1 NINC1 |+VE| .
SC EE ALADE 1 .
TRANS 820 MPLUR "PLURIEL" AACC .
SD % 1(N|+PLUR|,DEF|+PLUR|,V|+PLUR|,PRON|+PLUR|,
        QUEL|+PLUR|) % , WHERE 1 NINC1 |+VE| .
SC ES ALADE 1 .
    "TRANSFORMATIONS MORPHOPHONEMIQUES"
TRANS CONTPLUR "CONTRACTION PLURIEL" ACAC (DE LE ES) .
SD % DE 3LE 4(EE) ES % .
SC ERASE 3 , ERASE 4 .
TRANS ARTICLE ACAC (LE EE) .
SD % 2LE 3EE 4(ES) % .
SC ERASE 3 , IF <NUL 4> THEN <LA SUBSE 2> .
TRANS MCET "DEMONSTRATIF" ACAC (CET ES) .
SD % 2CET 3(EE) 4ES % .
SC ERASE 3 , ERASE 4 , CES SUBSE 2 .
CP IN LOWESTS(1) DO<I>; TREE; II .          $ENDTRA
$MAIN TRIN LEX TRAN.
```

```
EST-CE QUE TU AS REGARDE CETTE JOLIE FILLE?
  1 S          2 #
               3 PRE       4 INT
               5 SN        6 N        7 PERS
               8 SV        9 V       10 REGARD
                          11 SN      12 SN      13 DET    14 DEF     15 CET
                                                          16 CARD    17 UN
                                                18 N      19 FILLE
                                     20 S       22 #
                                                23 SN     24 DET     25 DEF     26 CET
                                                          27 CARD    28 UN
                                                          29 N       30 FILLE
                                                31 SV     32 V       33 JOLI
                                                34 #
              21 #

       #INT PERS REGARD CET UN FILLE#CET UN FILLE JOLI##
```

```
EST-CE CUE TU AS REGARDE CETTE JCLIE FILLE?
 1 S        2 #
            3 PRE     4 INT
            5 SN      6 N       7 PERS
            8 SV      9 V      10 REGARD
                     11 SN    12 SN       13 DET     14 DEF     15 CET
                                          16 CARD    17 UN
                              18 N        19 FILLE
                     2C S     22 #
                              23 SN       24 DET     25 DEF     26 CET
                                          27 CARD    28 UN
                                          29 N       30 FILLE
                              31 SV       32 V       33 JOLI
                              34 #
          21 #
```

```
           #INT PERS REGARD CET UN FILLE#CET UN FILLE JOLI##
     NODE       29
ANTEST CALLED FOR    101"      "(    )    ,SC=  2 . RESTRICTION=  C. TCP=  23:SN
ANTEST RETURNS ** 1**
     NODE       32
ANTEST CALLED FOR    105"      "(    )    ,SC=  6 . RESTRICTION=  0. TCP=  31:SV
ANTEST RETURNS ** 1**
ANTEST CALLED FOR    109"      "(    )    ,SD= 10 . RESTRICTION=  0. TCP=  20:S
ANTEST CALLED FOR    109"      "(    )    ,SC= 10 . RESTRICTION=  C. TCP=   1:S
     NODE       27
ANTEST CALLED FOR    103"      "(    )    ,SC=  4 . RESTRICTION=  0. TCP=  23:SN
ANTEST CALLED FOR    103"      "(    )    ,SD=  4 . RESTRICTION=  C. TCP=  11:SN
     NODE        6
ANTEST CALLED FOR    101"      "(    )    ,SD=  2 . RESTRICTION=  0. TCP=   5:SN
     NODE       18
ANTEST CALLED FOR    101"      "(    )    ,SC=  2 . RESTRICTION=  C. TCP=  12:SN
ANTEST RETURNS ** 1**
     NODE        9
ANTEST CALLED FOR    1C7"      "(    )    ,SC=  8 . RESTRICTION=  0. TOP=   8:SV
ANTEST RETURNS ** 1**
     NODE       16
ANTEST CALLED FOR    103"      "(    )    ,SC=  4 . RESTRICTION=  C. TCP=  12:SN
ANTEST CALLED FOR    103"      "(    )    ,SC=  4 . RESTRICTION=  0. TOP=  11:SN
```

```
EST-CE QUE TU AS REGARDE CETTE JOLIE FILLE?
  1 S            2 #
                 3 PRE      4 INT
                 5 SN       6 N       7 PERS
                 8 SV       9 V      10 REGARD
                           11 SN     12 SN      13 DET     14 DEF     15 CET
                                                           16 CARD    17 UN
                                      18 N      19 FILLE
                           20 S      22 #
                                      23 SN     24 DET     25 DEF     26 CET
                                                           27 CARD    28 UN
                                                 29 N      30 FILLE
                           31 SV     32 V       33 JOLI
                                      34 #
             21 #
NODE     6 N
         |+N -PLUR -FEM +EE +PERS -TWOPERS +HUM -<SN<DET_>>|
NODE     9 V
         |+V -FUTUR +PRET -PROG -<#S SV/<_%>%> +<SV/<_SN(ADVINS)>>|
NODE    16 CARD
         |+CARD -<SN/<%_N|+PLUR|>>|
NODE    18 N
         |+N -PLUR +FEM +EE +<SN<DET_>>|
NODE    27 CARD
         |+CARD -<SN/<%_N|+PLUR|>>|
NODE    29 N
         |+N -PLUR +FEM +EE +<SN<DET_>>|
NODE    32 V
         |+V +ADJ -FUTUR -FRET -PROG +FRENCH +<SV/<_>> -<S/<%_%ADVINS#>>|

         #INT PERS REGARD CET UN FILLE#CET UN FILLE JOLI##

*****      CONTROL PROGRAM      *****
SCAN CALLED AT       1      IN
SCAN CALLED AT       2      LOWESTS
SCAN CALLED AT       3      (
SCAN CALLED AT       4
SCAN CALLED AT       5      )
SCAN CALLED AT       6      DO
SCAN CALLED AT       7      <
ANTEST CALLED FOR      1"LOWESTS "(AC   )    ,SD= 13 . RESTRICTION=  3. TCP=   1:S
ANTEST CALLED FOR      1"LOWESTS "(AC   )    ,SC= 13 . RESTRICTION=  3. TCP=  20:S
ANTEST RETURNS ** 1**
SCAN CALLED AT       8      I
ANTEST CALLED FOR      8"ADJA1   "(AC   )    ,SD= 20 . RESTRICTION=  0. TCP=  20:S
ANTEST CALLED FOR      9"ADJA2   "(AC   )    ,SD= 21 . RESTRICTION=  0. TCP=  20:S
ANTEST CALLED FOR     10"ADJOE1  "(AC   )    ,SC= 22 . RESTRICTION=  C. TCP=  20:S
ANTEST CALLED FOR     11"ADJOE2  "(AC   )    ,SD= 23 . RESTRICTION=  0. TCP=  20:S
ANTEST CALLED FOR     15"ELLIOBJ "(AC   )    ,SC= 27 . RESTRICTION=  C. TCF=  20:S
ANTEST CALLED FOR     16"ACFRED  "(AC   )    ,SC= 28 . RESTRICTION=  C. TCP=  20:S
ANTEST RETURNS ** 1**
ANTEST CALLED FOR     17"REFLEXIF"(AC   )    ,SC= 29 . RESTRICTION=  8. TCP=  20:S
ANTEST CALLED FOR     19"ELLIPSE "(AC   )    ,SC= 31 . RESTRICTION=  0. TCP=  20:S
ANTEST RETURNS ** 1**
ELEMCP CALL FROM CHANGE - OPERATION,ARG1,ARG2 = ERASE          C      22
ELEMOP CALL FROM CHANGE - OPERATION,ARG1,ARG2 = ERASE          0      34
SCAN CALLED AT       9      >
ANTEST CALLED FOR      1"LOWESTS "(AC   )    ,SC= 13 . RESTRICTION=  3. TCP=   1:S
ANTEST RETURNS ** 1**
SCAN CALLED AT       8      I
```

```
ANTEST CALLED FOR     2"ACJCUE   "(AACC)    ,SC= 14 . RESTRICTION=  C. TOP=   1:S
ANTEST RETURNS ** 1**
ELEMCP CALL FRCM CHANGE - OPERATICN,ARG1,ARG2 = AFICE            35         2C
ANTEST CALLED FCR     3"ADJFROP "(AC  )     ,SC= 15 . RESTRICTION=  0. TOP=   1:S
ANTEST CALLED FCR     4"INFFROP "(AC  )     ,SC= 16 . RESTRICTION=  0. TCP=   1:S
ANTEST CALLED FCR     5"INFICENT"(AC  )     ,SC= 17 . RESTRICTION=  4. TOP=   1:S
ANTEST CALLED FOR     6"INFSUJ  "(AC  )     ,SC= 18 . RESTRICTICN=  5. TOP=   1:S
ANTEST CALLEC FCR     7"TRINF   "(AC  )     ,SC= 19 . RESTRICTION=  6. TCP=   1:S
ANTEST CALLED FOR     8"ACJA1   "(AC  )     ,SC= 20 . RESTRICTION=  0. TOP=   1:S
ANTEST CALLED FOR     9"ACJA2   "(AC  )     ,SC= 21 . RESTRICTION=  C. TCP=   1:S
ANTEST CALLEC FOR    10"ADJCE1  "(AC  )     ,SC= 22 . RESTRICTION=  C. TOP=   1:S
ANTEST CALLED FOR    11"ADJCE2  "(AC  )     ,SC= 23 . RESTRICTION=  0. TCP=   1:S
ANTEST CALLEC FOR    15"ELLIOBJ "(AC  )     ,SC= 27 . RESTRICTION=  0. TCP=   1:S
ANTEST CALLED FCR    16"ACFREC  "(AC  )     ,SC= 28 . RESTRICTION=  C. TCP=   1:S
ANTEST RETURNS ** 1**
ANTEST CALLED FOR    17"REFLEXIF"(AC  )     ,SC= 29 . RESTRICTION=  8. TCF=   1:S
ANTEST CALLED FCR    18"PRCNCM  "(ACAC)     ,SC= 30 . RESTRICTION=  9. TOP=   1:S
ANTEST RETURNS ** 1**
ELEMCP CALL FRCM CHANGE - CPERATICN,ARG1,ARG2 = SUBSE           36         24
ANTEST CALLED FCR    18"PRCNCM  "(ACAC)     ,SC= 30 . RESTRICTION=  9. TOP=   1:S
ANTEST CALLED FCR    19"ELLIPSE "(AC  )     ,SC= 31 . RESTRICTICN=  0. TCP=   1:S
ANTEST RETURNS ** 1**
ELEMCP CALL FRCM CHANGE - OPERATICN,ARG1,ARG2 = ERASE           0          2
ELEMCP CALL FROM CHANGE - CPERATICN,ARG1,ARG2 = ERASE           C          21
SCAN CALLEC AT       9    >
ANTEST CALLED FOR     1"LCWESTS "(AC  )     ,SC= 13 . RESTRICTION=  3. TCP=   1:S
ANTEST CALLED FOR     1"LCWESTS "(AC  )     ,SC= 13 . RESTRICTICN=  3. TCP=  20:S
SCAN CALLEC AT      10    ;
SCAN CALLEC AT      11    TREE
```

```
EST-CE QLE TU AS REGARDE CETTE JCLIE FILLE?
 1 S          3 PRE      4 INT
              5 SN       6 N         7 PERS
              8 SV       9 V        1C REGARD
             11 SN      12 SN       13 DET      14 DEF      15 CET
                                                16 CARD     17 UN
                                    18 N        19 FILLE
                         2C S       35 QUE
                                    23 SN       36 PRON
                                                29 N        30 FILLE
                                    31 SV       32 V        33 JOLI
NODE     6 N
         I+N -PLUR -FEM +EE +PERS -TWCPERS +HUM -<SN<DET_>>I
NODE     9 V
         I+V -PLUR -FEM +PERS -TWCPERS +VE -FUTUR +PRET -PROG -<#S SV/<_%>%> +<SV/<_SN(ADVINS)>>I
NODE    16 CARD
         I+CARD -<SN/<%_N|+PLUR|>>I
NODE    18 N
         I+N -PLUR +FEM +EE +<SN<DET_>>I
NODE    29 N
         I+N -PLUR +FEM +EE +<SN<DET_>>I
NODE    32 V
         I+V -PLUR +FEM +VE +ADJ -FUTUR -PRET -PROG +PRENOM +<SV/<_>> -<S/<%_%ADVINS#>>I

         INT PERS REGARD CET UN FILLE GLE FFCN FILLE JCLI
SCAN CALLEC AT      12     :
SCAN CALLEC AT      13     II
ANTEST CALLED FOR     20"RELATIF "(AACC)     ,SD= 32 . RESTRICTION= 10. TOP=     1:S
ANTEST RETLRNS ** 1**
ANTEST CALLED FCR     21"ACFRON  "(AACC)     ,SD= 33 . RESTRICTICN=  0. TCP=     1:S
ANTEST RETURNS ** 1**
ANTEST CALLED FCR     21"ACFRCN  "(AACC)     ,SD= 33 . RESTRICTICN=  0. TCP=    2C:S
ANTEST RETURNS ** 1**
ELEMCP CALL FRCM CHANCE - CPERATICN,ARG1,ARG2 = ERASE          C          25
ANTEST CALLED FOR     22"ACCLS   "(AC  )     ,SD= 34 . RESTRICTICN=  0. TOP=     1:S
ANTEST CALLED FOR     22"ACCUS   "(AC  )     ,SD= 34 . RESTRICTICN=  C. TCP=    20:S
ANTEST CALLED FCR     23"ACMINA  "(AC  )     ,SD= 35 . RESTRICTION=  0. TCP=     1:S
ANTEST RETLRNS ** 1**
ANTEST CALLED FOR     23"ACMINA  "(AC  )     ,SD= 35 . RESTRICTICN=  C. TCP=    20:S
ANTEST RETLRNS ** 1**
ANTEST CALLED FCR     24"ELLIDET "(AACC)     ,SD= 36 . RESTRICTION= 13. TCF=     1:S
ANTEST CALLEC FCR     25"ELLISING"(AACC)     ,SD= 37 . RESTRICTICN=  0. TCF=     1:S
ANTEST RETLRNS ** 1**
ELEMCP CALL FRCM CHANGE - CPERATICN,ARG1,ARG2 = ERASE          C          16
ANTEST CALLEC FCR     26"RECREL  "(AACC)     ,SD= 38 . RESTRICTICN=  C. TOP=    2C:S
ANTEST RETURNS ** 1**
ELEMCP CALL FRCM CHANGE - CPERATICN,ARG1,ARG2 = ADLES         32          20
FLEMOP CALL FRCM CHANGE - CPERATICN,ARG1,ARG2 = ERASE          0          2C
ANTEST CALLED FOR     27"ELLICCMP"(ACAC)     ,SC= 39 . RESTRICTION= 15. TCP=     1:S
ANTEST CALLED FCR     28"MDEM    "(AACC)     ,SD= 4C . RESTRICTICN=  0. TCP=     1:S
ANTEST CALLED FCR     31"ANTEPC1 "(AC  )     ,SC= 43 . RESTRICTICN=  0. TOP=     1:S
ANTEST CALLED FCR     34"ANTEPAJ "(AACC)     ,SD= 46 . RESTRICTION= 22. TCF=     1:S
ANTEST RETURNS ** 1**
ELEMCP CALL FRCM CHANCE - CPERATICN,ARC1,ARG2 = ALESE         37          18
ELEMCP CALL FRCM CHANCE - OPERATION,ARG1,ARG2 = SUBSE         12          11
ANTEST CALLED FCR     41"MPASS   "(AC  )     ,SC= 53 . RESTRICTION=  C. TOP=     1:S
ANTEST CALLED FCR     42"MSLBJ   "(AC  )     ,SC= 54 . RESTRICTION=  0. TOP=     1:S
ANTEST CALLEC FCR     43"IMPAR   "(AC  )     ,SC= 55 . RESTRICTICN= 25. TCP=     1:S
ANTEST CALLED FCR     44"METREPAS"(AC  )     ,SC= 56 . RESTRICTION= 26. TOP=     1:S
ANTEST CALLED FCR     45"MAVCIPAS"(AC  )     ,SD= 57 . RESTRICTICN=  0. TCP=     1:S
```

```
ANTEST RETURNS ** 1**
ELEMCP CALL FROM CHANGE - OPERATION,ARG1,ARG2 = AFIDE          35         40
ELEMCP CALL FROM CHANGE - OPERATION,ARG1,ARG2 = ARISE          41         10
ANTEST CALLED FOR     46"MINF    "(AC  )   ,SC= 58 . RESTRICTION=  0. TOP=    1:S
ANTEST CALLED FOR     47"MFUTUR  "(AC  )   ,SC= 59 . RESTRICTION=  0. TOP=    1:S
ANTEST CALLED FOR     48"ACCPPO  "(AC  )   ,SC= 60 . RESTRICTION=  0. TOP=    1:S
ANTEST CALLED FOR     50"PREVPRO "(AC  )   ,SC= 62 . RESTRICTION=  0. TOP=    1:S
ANTEST CALLED FOR     51"PCSTPRO "(ACAC)   ,SC= 63 . RESTRICTION= 29. TOP=    1:S
ANTEST CALLED FOR     52"NOMACCPR"(AACC)   ,SC= 64 . RESTRICTION= 31. TOP=    1:S
ANTEST RETURNS ** 1**
ELEMCP CALL FROM CHANGE - OPERATION,ARG1,ARG2 = SUBSE          42          7
ANTEST CALLED FOR     53"GNPRON  "(AACC)   ,SC= 65 . RESTRICTION=  0. TOP=    1:S
ANTEST CALLED FOR     54"ADJESK  "(AC  )   ,SC= 66 . RESTRICTION= 35. TOP=    1:S
ANTEST RETURNS ** 1**
ELEMCP CALL FROM CHANGE - OPERATION,ARG1,ARG2 = ALADE          44          4
ELEMCP CALL FROM CHANGE - OPERATION,ARG1,ARG2 = ALADE          45          4
ANTEST CALLED FOR     55"ADJSI   "(AC  )   ,SC= 67 . RESTRICTION= 36. TOP=    1:S
ANTEST CALLED FOR     57"NOMACCIN"(ACAC)   ,SC= 69 . RESTRICTION=  0. TOP=    1:S
ANTEST RETURNS ** 1**
ELEMCP CALL FROM CHANGE - OPERATION,ARG1,ARG2 = ALESE          46         45
ELEMCP CALL FROM CHANGE - OPERATION,ARG1,ARG2 = SUBSE          47         45
ANTEST CALLED FOR     57"NOMACCIN"(ACAC)   ,SC= 69 . RESTRICTION=  0. TOP=    1:S
ANTEST CALLED FOR     63"MFEM    "(AACC)   ,SC= 75 . RESTRICTION= 42. TOP=    1:S
ANTEST RETURNS ** 2**
ELEMCP CALL FROM CHANGE - OPERATION,ARG1,ARG2 = ALADE          48         14
ELEMCP CALL FROM CHANGE - OPERATION,ARG1,ARG2 = ALADE          45         37
ANTEST CALLED FOR     64"MPLUR   "(AACC)   ,SC= 76 . RESTRICTION= 43. TOP=    1:S
SCAN CALLED AT    14      .
```

```
TRANSFORMATIONS WHICH HAVE APPLIED ARE
         1        1   LOWESTS
         2       16   ACPRED
         3       19   ELLIPSE
         4        1   LOWESTS
         5        2   ADJQUE
         6       16   ACPRED
         7       18   PRONOM
         8       19   ELLIPSE
         9       20   RELATIF
        10       21   ACPRON
        11       23   NOMINA
        12       25   ELLISING
        13       26   REDREL
        14       34   ANTEPAJ
        15       45   MAVCIPAS
        16       52   NOMACCPR
        17       54   ADJESK
        18       57   NOMACCIN
        19       63   MFEM
```

```
EST-CE QUE TU AS REGARDE CETTE JOLIE FILLE?
  1 S              3 PRE       4 INT      44 EST
                                          46 CE
                                          47 QUE
                 5 SN          6 N        42 JE
                 8 SV         40 V        39 AV
                                           9 V         10 REGARD
                                          41 E
                12 SN         13 DET      14 DEF       15 CET
                                                       48 EE
                              37 V        38 JOLI
                                          49 EE
                              18 N        19 FILLE
NODE      6 N
          |+N -PLUR -FEM +EE +PERS -TWOPERS +HUM +NOMIN -<SN<DET_>>|
NODE     40 V
          |+V -PLUR -FEM +PERS -TWOPERS +VE -FUTUR -<#S SV/<_%>%> +<SV/<_SN(ADVINS)>>|
NODE      9 V
          |+V|
NODE     14 DEF
          |-PLUR +FEM +EMP|
NODE     37 V
          |+V -PLUR +FEM +ADJ +PRENOM +<SV/<_>> -<S/<%_%ADVINS#>>|
NODE     18 N
          |+N -PLUR +FEM +EE +EMP +<SN<DET_>>|

          EST CE QUE JE AV REGARD E CET EE JOLI EE FILLE

TRIN. NO MORE INPUTS.
```

Complete Syntax for Transformational Grammar

0.01 *transformational-grammar* ::= *phrase-structure lexicon transformations* $

1.01 *tree* ::= *node* opt[*complex-symbol*] opt[⟨ list[*tree*] ⟩]

1.02 *node* ::= *word* [] *sentence-symbol* [] *boundary-symbol*

1.03 *sentence-symbol* ::= **S**

1.04 *boundary-symbol* ::= #

2.01 *structural-description* ::= *structural-analysis* opt[, **WHERE** *restriction*]

2.02 *contextual-feature-description* ::= ⟨ *structure* opt[, **WHERE** *restriction*] ⟩

2.03 *structural-analysis* ::= list[*term*]

2.04 *term* ::= opt[*integer*] *structure* [] opt[*integer*] *choice* [] *skip*

2.05 *structure* ::= *element* opt[*complex-symbol*] opt[opt[⌐] opt[/] ⟨ *structural-analysis* ⟩]

2.06 *element* ::= *node* [] * [] _

2.07 *choice* ::= (clist[*structural-analysis*])

2.08 *skip* ::= %

3.01 *restriction* ::= **booleancombination**[*condition*]

3.02 *condition* ::= *unary-condition* [] *binary-condition*

3.03 *unary-condition* ::= *unary-relation integer*

3.04 *binary-condition* ::= *integer binary-tree-relation node-designator* []
      integer binary-complex-relation complex-symbol-designator

3.05   *node-designator* ::= *integer* □ *node*

3.06   *complex-symbol-designator* ::= *complex-symbol* □ *integer*

3.07   *unary-relation* ::= TRM □ NTRM □ NUL □ NNUL

3.08   *binary-tree-relation* ::= EQ □ NEQ □ DOM □ NDOM □ DOMS □ NDOMS □ DOMBY □ NDOMBY □

3.09   *binary-complex-relation* ::= INC1 □ NINC1 □ INC2 □ NINC2 □ CSEQ □ NCSEQ □ NDST □ NNDST □
        COMP □ NCOMP

4.01   *complex-symbol* ::= | list[*feature-specification*] |

4.02   *feature-specification* ::= *value feature*

4.03   *feature* ::= *category-feature* □ *inherent-feature* □ *contextual-feature*

4.04   *category-feature* ::= *word*

4.05   *inherent-feature* ::= *word*

4.06   *contextual-feature* ::= *word*

4.07   *value* ::= + □ – □ *

5.01   *structural-change* ::= clist[*change-instruction*]

5.02   *change-instruction* ::= *change* □ *conditional-change*

5.03   *conditional-change* ::= IF ⟨ *restriction* ⟩ THEN ⟨ *structural-change* ⟩ opt[ELSE ⟨ *structural-change* ⟩]

5.04   *change* ::= *unary-operator integer* □ *tree-designator binary-tree-operator integer* □
        complex-symbol-designator binary-complex-operator integer □
        complex-symbol-designator ternary-complex-operator integer integer

5.05   *tree-designator* ::= (*tree*) □ *node* □ *integer*

5.06   *unary-operator* ::= ERASE □ ERASEI

5.07   *binary-tree-operator* ::= ADLAD □ ALADE □ ADLADI □ ALADEI □ ADFID □ AFIDE □ ADRIS □
        ARISE □ ADRISI □ ARISEI □ ADLES □ ALESE □ ADLESI □ ALESEI □ ADRIA □ ARIAE □
        SUBST □ SUBSE □ SUBSTI □ SUBSEI □ ADCHL □ ACHLE □ ADCHR □ ACHRE □

5.08   *binary-complex-operator* ::= ERASEF □ MERGEF □ SAVEF

5.09   *ternary-complex-operator* ::= **MOVEF**

6.01   *phrase-structure* ::= **PHRASESTRUCTURE** list[*phrase-structure-rule*] **$**

6.02   *phrase-structure-rule* ::= *rule-left* = *rule-right* .

6.03   *rule-left* ::= *node*

6.04   *rule-right* ::= *node* [] list[*rule-right*] [] (clist[*rule-right*])

7.01   *lexicon* ::= **LEXICON** *prelexicon lexical-entries* **$**

7.02   *prelexicon* ::= *feature-definitions* opt[*redundancy-rules*]

7.03   *feature-definitions* ::= *category-definitions* opt[*inherent-definitions*] opt[*contextual-definitions*]

7.04   *category-definitions* ::= **CATEGORY** list[*category-feature*] .

7.05   *inherent-definitions* ::= **INHERENT** list[*inherent-feature*] .

7.06   *contextual-definitions* ::= **CONTEXTUAL** clist[*contextual-definition*] .

7.07   *contextual-definition* ::= *contextual-feature* = *contextual-feature-description*

7.08   *redundancy-rules* ::= **RULES** clist[*redundancy-rule*] .

7.09   *redundancy-rule* ::= *complex-symbol* => *complex-symbol*

7.10   *lexical-entries* ::= **ENTRIES** clist[*lexical-entry*] .

7.11   *lexical-entry* ::= list[*vocabulary-word*] list[*complex-symbol*]

7.12   *vocabulary-word* ::= *word*

8.01   *transformations* ::= **TRANSFORMATIONS** list[*transformation*] **CP** *control-program* . **$**

8.02   *transformation* ::= **TRANS** *identification* . **SD** *structural-description* . opt[**SC** *structural-change*] .

8.03   *identification* ::= opt[*integer*] *transformation-name* opt[list[*parameter*]] opt[*keywords*]

8.04   *transformation-name* ::= *word*

8.05   *parameter* ::= *group-number* [] *optionality* [] *repetition*

8.06   *group-number* ::= **I** [] **II** [] **III** [] **IV** [] **V** [] **VI** [] **VII**

8.07   *optionality* ::= **OB** □ **OP**

8.08   *repetition* ::= **AC** □ **ACAC** □ **AACC** □ **AAC**

8.09   *keywords* ::= (**list**[*node*])

9.01   *control-program* ::= **sclist**[**opt**[*label* :] *instruction*]

9.02   *label* ::= *word*

9.03   *instruction* ::= *transformation-element* □ *control-element* □ ⟨ **sclist**[*instruction*] ⟩

9.04   *transformation-element* ::= *transformation-name* □ *group-number*

9.05   *control-element* ::= *IN-instruction* □ *RPT-instruction* □ *IF-instruction* □ *FLAG-instruction* □ *GOTO-instruction* □ *TRACE-instruction* □ *STOP-instruction*

9.06   *IN-instruction* ::= **IN** *transformation-name* (*integer*) **DO** ⟨ *control-program* ⟩

9.07   *RPT-instruction* ::= **RPT** **opt**[*integer*]⟨ *control-program* ⟩

9.08   *IF-instruction* ::= **IF** *instruction* **THEN** *GOTO-instruction* **opt**[**ELSE** *GOTO-instruction*] □ **IF** *FLAG-name* **THEN** *GOTO-instruction* **opt**[**ELSE** *GOTO-instruction*]

9.09   *FLAG-instruction* ::= *FLAG-name* *transformation-list*

9.10   *FLAG-name* ::= **FLAG** **opt**[*integer*]

9.11   *transformation-list* ::= *transformation-element* □ ⟨ **sclist**[*transformation-element*] ⟩

9.12   *GOTO-instruction* ::= **GOTO** *label*

9.13   *TRACE-instruction* ::= **TRACE** *transformation-list* *trace-specification* □ **UNTRACE** *transformation-list* *trace-specification* □ **AFTER CHANGE TREE**

9.14   *trace-specification* ::= **BEFORE TEST** □ **AFTER SUCCESS** □ **AFTER FAILURE**

9.15   *STOP-instruction* ::= **STOP**

CROSS-INDEX TO SYNTAX RULES

The index gives the rules in which the format occurs on the right.

References

Backus, J.W. "The Syntax and Semantics of the Proposed International Algebraic Language of the Zurich ACM-GAMM Conference," *Proc. 1st International Conference Information Processing, UNESCO, Paris, 1959.* London, 1960.

Blair, F. "Programming of the Grammar Tester," in *Specification and Utilization of a Transformational Grammar,* ed. D. Lieberman, IBM Watson Research Center, Yorktown Heights, N.Y., 1966.

Chomsky, N. *Syntactic Structures,* The Hague: 1957.

Chomsky, N. *Aspects of the Theory of Syntax,* Cambridge, Mass. 1965.

Chomsky, N. "Remarks on Nominalization," in *Readings in English Transformational Grammar,* eds. P. S. Rosenbaum and R. Jacobs, Waltham, Mass. (forthcoming).

Doran, Robert W. 360 O.S. FORTRAN IV Free-field Input/output Subroutine Package, CS-79, Computer Science Department, Stanford University, 1967.

Fillmore, C. J. "The Position of Embedding Transformations in a Grammar," *Word,* 19 (1963), 208-231.

Friedman, Joyce. SYNN, An Experimental Analysis Program for Transformational Grammars, WP-229, The MITRE Corporation, 1965.

Friedman, Joyce. "Directed Random Generation of Sentences," *Communications of the ACM,* 12 (1969), 40-46.

Friedman, Joyce. "A Computer System for Transformational Grammar," *Communications of the ACM,* 12 (1969), 341-348.

Friedman, Joyce, ed. Computer Experiments in Transformational Grammar, CS-108, Computer Science Department, Stanford University, 1968.

Friedman, Joyce *et al.* Programmers' Manual for a Computer System for Transformational Grammar, CS-115, Computer Science Department, Stanford University, 1968.

Gross, L. N. On-line Programming System User's Manual, MTP-59, The MITRE Corporation, 1967.

Gross, L. N. MIT Rule Tester, mimeographed, 1968.

Hill, Kenneth C. A Grammar of the Serrano Language, Ph.D. Dissertation, University of California, Los Angeles, 1967.

Klevansky, Lorraine. A transformational grammar for Swahili, AF-32, Computer Science Department, Stanford University, 1968.

Klima, E. S. "Current Developments in Generative Grammar," *Kybernetika,* 1 (1965), 184-197.

Lakoff, G. On the Nature of Syntactic Irregularity, NSF-16, The Computation Laboratory, Harvard University, 1965.

Lees, R. B. *A Grammar of English Nominalizations,* Supplement to *International Journal of American Linguistics,* Baltimore, 1960.

Lieberman, D., ed. *Specification and Utilization of a Transformational Grammar,* IBM Watson Research Center, Yorktown Heights, N.Y., 1966.

Lieberman, D. "Design of a grammar tester," in *Specification and Utilization of a Transformational Grammar,* ibid.

Londe, D. L. and W. J. Schoene, TGT: Transformational Grammar Tester, *Proc. Spring Joint Computer Conference,* 1968, Part I, 385-393.

Morin, Yves Ch. Computer Experiments in Transformational Grammar: French I, Report NLS 3, Ann Arbor, 1969.

Nagara, Susumu and Donald L. Smith, Computer Experiments in Transformational Grammar: Japanese, multilithed, Ann Arbor, 1970.

Naur, P., ed. "Report on the Algorithmic Language ALGOL 60," *Communications of the ACM,* 3 (1960), 299-314.

Partee, Barbara H., P. Schachter, R. Stockwell, *et al.* Working Papers, U.C.L.A.— Air Force English Syntax Conference, multilithed, 1967.

Partee, Barbara Hall. Computer Tests of AFESP Case Grammar 1, Working paper 23, English Syntax Project, U.C.L.A., 1968.

Perlmutter, David M. Deep and Surface Contraints in Syntax, Ph.D. Dissertation, Massachusetts Institute of Technology, Cambridge, Mass., 1968.

Petrick, Stanley R. A Recognition Procedure for Transformational Grammars, Ph.D. Dissertation, Massachusetts Institute of Technology, Cambridge, Mass., 1965.

Postal, Paul M. "Cross-Over Phenomena," in *Specification and Utilization of a Transformational Grammar,* Scientific Report No. 3, IBM Watson Research Center, Yorktown Heights, N.Y., 1968.

Querido, Antonio A. M. Grammaire I, description transformationelle d'un sous-ensemble du français, International Conference on Computational Linguistics, Sånga-Säby, Sweden, preprint No. 43, 1969.

Rosenbaum, P., and Dorita Lochak, "The IBM Core Grammar of English," in *Specification and Utilization of a Transformational Grammar,* ed. D. Lieberman.

Ross, J. R. A proposed rule of tree-pruning, NSF-17, Computation Laboratory, Harvard University, IV-1-18, 1966.

Ross J. R. Constraints on Variables in Syntax, Ph.D. Dissertation, Massachusetts Institute of Technology, Cambridge, Mass. 1967.

Stockwell, R., P. Schachter, Barbara Partee, *et al.* Working papers of the English Syntax Project, U.C.L.A., mimeographed, 1967.

Traugott, Elizabeth Closs. Deep and Surface Structure in Alfredian Prose, mimeographed, 1967, PEGS.

Zwicky, A. M., Joyce Friedman, Barbara C. Hall, and D. E. Walker, "The MITRE Syntactic Analysis Procedure for Transformational Grammars," *Proc. Fall Joint Computer Conference,* 1965, Vol. 27, Pt. 1, 317-326.

Zwicky, A. M. On the Ordering of Embedding Transformations, Mimeographed handout, Meeting of the Linguistic Society of America, 1966.

Index

With key to mnemonics

NOTE: A cross-index to the syntax rules appears as the second part of Appendix B.